HISTORY
OF THE EARTH

GEOLOGY ECOLOGY BIOLOGY

BARRON'S

DoGi

First edition for the United States and Canada published 2003 by Barron's Educational Series, Inc.

Original title: *La grande storia della Terra*
Copyright © 2002 by DoGi SpA—Italy

Text
Yuri Castelfrsanchi and Nico Pitrelli

Graphic Display
Andrea Rauch

Science Consultant
Barbara Gallavotti

Page make-up
Sansai Zappini

Editor
Francesco Milo

English translation
Jeremy Carden

Illustrations
Gian Paolo Faleschini
Leonardo Meschini

Printed by Eurolitho SpA
Cesano Boscone (Milan)
© 2002 by DoGi SpA, Italy
COD.

All inquiries should be addressed to:
Barron's Educational Series, Inc.
250 Wireless Boulevard
Hauppauge, New York 11788
http://www.barronseduc.com

International Standard Book Number 0-7641-5680-2
Library of Congress Catalog Card Number: 2003100374

PRINTED IN ITALY
9 8 7 6 5 4 3 2 1

Acknowledgments

The illustrations in this volume have been realized in accordance with a project developed by DoGi Spa, which owns the copyright.
Abbreviations: t: top; b: bottom; c: center; r: right; l: left.

Illustrations:
Alessandro Baldanzi: 91t, 105t; Alessandro Bartolozzi: 8-9c, 16, 18b, 19t, 21l, 24t, 25tl, 55b, 85tr; Archivio DoGi: 23r, 25br, 25tr, 28, 33c, 43r, 50t, 53, 56, 59cr, 60t, 71bl, 74, 74t, 76t, 79b, 96cl, 110-111, 118-119; Remo Borselli: 59t; Luca Cascioli: 23l, 30c, 98tc; Lorenzo Cecchi: 41l, 75br; Adriano Ciuffetti: 112; Luciano Crovato and Gianni Mazzoleni: 96t, 12b; Gian Paolo Faleschini: 40, 47 62, 63, 69, 78-79, 78t, 79r; Gian Paolo Faleschini with the help of Edoardo Marinelli: 10-11, 11tr, 14-15, 32, 34-35, 36-37, 50-51, 60-61, 64-65, 66-67, 68, 71t, 72-73, 76-77, 88-89, 92-93, 102-103, 104-105, 106-107, 108-109, 117tr; Gian Gian Paolo Faleschini with the help of Leonardo Meschini: 26-27, 27tr, 29b, 41t, 41l, 38, 46-47, 52t, 57tc, 58-59, 59b, 70, 71t, 80; Raffaele Ferrante: 48, 91cr; Giuliano Fornari: 86
Paola Holguin: 120; Bernardo Mannucci: 10; Alessandro Menchi: 106b; Leonardo Meschini: 17, 21r, 33b, 37c, 43l, 44-45, 49, 52b, 54-55, 56t, 57b, 118tl, 119cr; Alessandra Micheletti: 81br; Francesco Spadoni: 20bl, 22t, 30t, 75c, 82t, 82b, 99, 100t, 116l; Studio Caba: 114; Sauro Giampaia: 71br; Inklink, Florence: 42, 67cr, 83cr, 84-85, 94, 100-101, 114, 121t; Lorenzo Orlandi: 98b; Laura Ottina: 24c; Raimondo Pasin: 81cl; Francesco Petracchi: 20r, 44t, 56cr, 86; Sergio: 29t, 82-83, 83t, 90, 95t; Sebastiano Ranchetti: 8; Sansai Zappini: 12t, 18t, 19c, 20cl, 22c, 25b, 31, 39t, 55t, 97, 113, 116-117.

Computer Artworks:
Sansai Zappini

Reproductions and documents
DoGi SpA has done its best to discover possible rights of third parties. We apologize for any omissions or mistakes that may have occurred, and we will be pleased to introduce the appropriate corrections in later editions of this book.

Cover:
Gian Paolo Faleschini
Inside:
NASA: 8-9t; Archivio DoGi: 12cl, 13t, 13r, 17t, 23b; 40, 41, 49, 68, 69, 77, 80, 81, 84, 86, 87, 99, 103t, 110, 111, 113, 114, 115; Alessio Argentieri: 121; Associated Press: 17r; CNRI-Overseas: 12bl; double's/Holt Studios International/Nigel Cattlin: 94; double's: 105; Farabolafoto-Overseas/M. Wendlen: 119; K&G/Valsecchi: 12bl, 13bl, 13c, 26t; Giuliano Milo: 66; The Image Bank, Roma/L.D. Gordon: 90; The Natural History Museum: 61, 70; Naturhistorisches Museum, Vienna: 91; Overseas/A. Sferlazzo: 43; Panda Photo/R.Siniscalchi: 28t; Overseas-Oxford Scientific Films/Mark Deeble & Victoria Stone: 32; Overseas-Oxford Scientific Films/M.P.L. Fogden: 67; Overseas/Bob Zola: 97; Oversea-Explorer/Eric Schings: 103b; Overseas-Explorer/F. Gohier: 112; Panda Photo/C. Galasso: 37; Panda Photo/A. Petretti: 45; Panda Photo/S. Ardito: 101; Panda Photo-FLPA/M. Callan: 105; Panda Photo/J.C. Munoz: 107; Panda Photo/R. Faidutti:118.

Contents

8 The young Earth

10 *The primordial dust*
13 *The iron core*
16 *The formation of the atmosphere and the oceans*
19 *The birth of life*
21 *What's for dinner?*
22 *Oxygen: vital or lethal?*

The explosion of life 26

Two motors of evolution: chance and necessity 28
Strength in union 30
The advantages of sexual reproduction 30
The Cambrian explosion 33
The birth of vertebrates 37
The move to dry land 39
A revolutionary jaw 40
Amphibians and forests 42
The Permian 45
The catastrophe of the Permian 47

50 The age of the dinosaurs

53 *After the disaster … life*
54 *From reptiles to mammals*
58 *The arrival of the "terrible lizards"*
62 *Major developments: feathers and flowers*
67 *Major innovations in the Cretaceous*
70 *Dying giants*

The triumph of mammals 72

The development of mammals in the Cenozoic 75
Parental care and reproductive strategies 77
On land and in the sea 78
From the first primates to humans 81
The achievements of Homo sapiens 90

92 Humans and the planet

94 *An animal with a thousand habitats*
96 *Life in the city*
99 *Environments*
116 *Looking to the future*

Thematic table of contents

The history of life

18 The first living organisms
20 DNA, RNA, proteins, and the genetic code
22 Autotrophs and heterotrophs
24 Present-day cells
28 Evolution
34 **In the waters of the Cambrian**
36 The primitive oceans
40 The fish age
42 The first vascular plants
44 The first terrestrial vertebrates
46 The Carboniferous forests
52 Reptiles
54 Therapsids
56 Dinosaurs
58 Parental care among dinosaurs
60 The major dinosaur beds
62 Pterosaurs and ichthyosaurs
64 **Dinosaurs on the hunt**
66 The blossoming of the first flowers
68 The extinction of the dinosaurs
70 Birds
74 Mammals and adaptive radiation
76 Messel: a complete ecosystem
78 Carnivores and herbivores
80 The early primates
82 The genus *Homo*
84 Out of Africa
88 **The weapons of *Homo sapiens***
90 The development of farming

Ecology

94 The biosphere and biodiversity
96 The cycles of the biosphere
98 The major natural environments
100 Polar regions
102 The northern forests
104 Mediterranean environments
106 Savannas and grasslands
108 **The tropical forests**
110 Islands
114 Fires
118 The last major extinction
120 Sustainable development

Geology and climate

10 The structure of the Earth and the terrestrial crust
12 The formation of rocks
14 **The landscape of primordial Earth**
16 Volcanoes and eruptions
30 The dance of the tectonic plates
32 Rivers, lakes, mountains
38 Fossils: how they form, how they are dated
48 The origin of oil and coal
86 Ice ages
112 Earthquakes
116 Climatic changes

How to read this book

Chapter heading
Each of the five chapters opens with a
double-page spread. The text at the top left is
an introduction to the running text in the
pages that follow.

Figures
The illustrations and accompanying notes
provide information that is particularly useful
for understanding the themes of the chapter.

Color-coded contents bar
At a glance you can see which major subject
area is being covered on a given double page:
Red is for the history of life, blue is for geology
and climate, and green is for ecology.

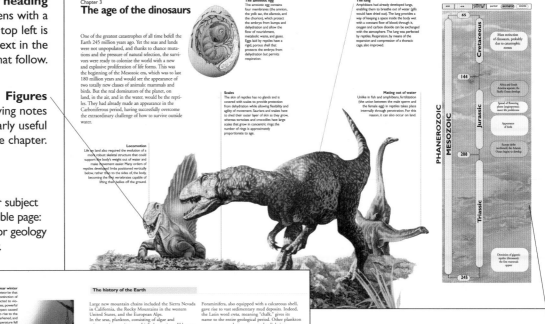

One of the greatest catastrophes of all time befell the
Earth 245 million years ago. Yet the seas and lands
were not unpopulated, and thanks to chance mutations and the pressure of natural selection, the survivors were ready to colonize the world with a new
and explosive proliferation of life forms. This was
the beginning of the Mesozoic era, which was to last
180 million years and would see the appearance of
two totally new classes of animals: mammals and
birds. But the real dominators of the planet, on
land, in the air, and in the water, would be the reptiles. They had already made an appearance in the
Carboniferous period, having successfully overcome
the extraordinary challenge of how to survive outside
water.

The amniotic egg
The amniotic egg contains
four membranes (the amnion,
the yolk sac, the allantois, and
the chorion), which protect
the embryo from bumps and
dehydration and allow the
flow of nourishment,
metabolic waste, and gases.
Eggs laid by reptiles have a
rigid, porous shell that
protects the embryo from
dehydration but permits
respiration.

The lung
Amphibians had already developed lungs,
enabling them to breathe out of water (gills
would have dried out). The lung provides a
way of keeping a steady state inside the body wet
with a constant flow of blood; through it,
oxygen and carbon dioxide can be exchanged
with the atmosphere. The lung was perfected
by reptiles. Respiration, by means of the
expansion and compression of a thoracic
cage, also improved.

Scales
The skin of reptiles has no glands and is
covered with scales to provide protection
from dehydration while allowing flexibility and
agility of movement. Saurians and snakes have
to shed their outer layer of skin as they grow,
whereas tortoises and crocodiles have large
scales that grow in concentric rings; the
number of rings is approximately
proportionate to age.

Mating out of water
Unlike in fish and amphibians, fertilization
(the union between the male sperm and
the female egg) in reptiles takes place
internally through penetration. For this
reason, it can also occur on land.

Locomotion
Life on land also required the evolution of a
more robust skeletal structure that could
support the body's weight out of water and
make movement easier. Many orders of
reptiles developed limbs positioned vertically
below, rather than to the sides of, the body,
becoming the first vertebrates capable of
lifting their bellies off the ground.

Chronology
Each double-page spread introduction is
accompanied by a chronological time chart
summing up the main geological and
biological events in the history of the Earth.

Running text
Page after page you can read about the history
of the Earth and the evolution of life from its
origins to the present day.

The frontiers of knowledge
A series of boxes focusing on some of the
unresolved questions, new theories, recent
discoveries, and most urgent problems being
debated by scientists.

The extinction of the dinosaurs

The most accredited current hypothesis to explain the
extinction of the dinosaurs is that the Earth was struck by a
meteorite, but there is no lack of objections to this theory.
Some scientists emphasize the improbability that just one
meteorite, however big, produced an ecological catastrophe
leading to the extinction not only of dinosaurs but also of
nearly two thirds of all living species. The disappearance of
dinosaurs might have been caused by a typical set of ecological
dynamics that have been used to explain previous extinctions.
It is possible, for instance, that the separation of the
continents and the consequent
change in climate led to
the disappearance of
many specific ecological
niches to which
dinosaurs had
adapted.

Nuclear winter
After the impact of the meteorite that
hypothetically caused the extinction of
dinosaurs, the Earth was subjected to violent earthquakes and seaquakes, powerful
winds, and acid rain. The impact caused
columns of smoke and dust to rise to the
upper atmosphere. The sky darkened, and
the temperature fell
dramatically, radically upsetting the
climatic balance. The planet remained
cold and dark for many years.

The history of the Earth

Large new mountain chains included the Sierra Nevada
in California, the Rocky Mountains in the western
United States, and the European Alps.
In the seas, plankton, consisting of algae and
microscopic organisms, multiplied at an incredible rate.
Some species of single-cell algae secreted a kind of
spherical calcareous skeleton consisting of small, oval
platelets called coccoliths. For millions of years, the
abundant calcareous remains of these algae deposited
on the seabed. When the sea level dropped at the end
of the Cretaceous, these deposits formed immense
blocks of chalky rocks along coasts. The most famous
ones are the white cliffs of Dover in England.

Foraminifera, also equipped with a calcareous shell,
gave rise to vast sedimentary mud deposits. Indeed,
the Latin word creta, meaning "chalk," gives its
name to the entire geological period. Other plankton
components, such as sponges and radiolarians,
developed siliceous spicules or shells. Their corpses
accumulated on the ocean floor, resulting in chert
beds.
Toward the end of the Cretaceous, the sea level began
to drop rapidly and the continents reemerged. Animals
and plants were ready to colonize the immense
expanses of land. But then, once again, the Earth
was struck by a major catastrophe.

THE CATASTROPHE THEORY

*In 1978, the American geologist Walter Alvarez made a
discovery in the clay of the Scaglia Rossa, a succession of
sedimentary rocks found in various places on the Earth's
surface. He found that the clay had an abnormally high
content of iridium, a chemical element that is very rare
on Earth but which is present in asteroids. The stratum of
red clay marks the geological boundary between the
Cretaceous and the Paleocene and conserves clear signs of
the extinction. Alvarez had thus found evidence in favor
of his thesis that the disappearance of dinosaurs was caused by a meteorite. Subsequently, a crater where the
impact was thought to have taken place was
discovered off the Yucatan peninsula in Mexico.*

The survivors
According to the meteorite
theory, dinosaurs disappeared
because they were unable
to survive the tough "nuclear
winter." The life forms that
managed to survive these extreme
conditions were organisms living
in the ocean depths, plants
resistant to the cold, and animals
that weighed less than 55 pounds
(25 kg) and were thus better able
to tolerate temperature swings.

Polar dinosaurs
Fossil remains appear to show that some
dinosaurs even adapted to living in very cold
climates near the poles. These were generally
small and almost certainly warm-blooded
herbivores and carnivores.

JURASSIC PARK

*Science does not exclude the possibility
of being able to use DNA to recreate
a dinosaur or even a whole park of
enormous Mesozoic reptiles,
as presented in Steven Spielberg's movie
Jurassic Park. All this would be possible
through cloning, a genetic engineering
technique that can be used to
reproduce millions of copies of determinate
regions of DNA. However, a cloning project
like this would require something that has
not yet been found, namely, a fossil with
organic tissue containing, almost intact, the
precious genetic material. For now it only
happens in movies.*

Stories and pioneers of science
A series of boxes relating the stories of women,
men, and great discoveries that have made a
major contribution to scientific research.

Dinosaurs on the hunt

*Dinosaurs developed various hunting techniques. It is not easy
to reconstruct them, but some help comes from fossil remains,
especially ones that include both prey and predator, traces of
wounds on the bones of large herbivores, and tracks from which
one can reconstruct an entire hunting scenario. Some dinosaurs
were solitary predators who stalked their prey or lay in ambush.
Others organized themselves into groups to kill large herbivores
or to surround those that lived in small packs.*

What color were they?
Giant dinosaurs had no need either to
draw attention to or to camouflage
themselves and were probably neutral in
color. Smaller dinosaurs would have used
camouflage colors, but in the mating season
the males might have displayed colored
stripes or patches. Poisonous or disgusting
animals may have had bright colors to ward
off attackers. The coloring of some species
may have helped to regulate body
temperature: Light colors reflect the heat;
dark ones absorb it.

The intelligence of dinosaurs
Some paleontologists have even gone so
far as to estimate the IQ of dinosaurs:
their deductions are based on the size of
the animals' brains in relation to body
mass and lifestyle. The most stupid were
sauropods, whereas Velociraptor and
Deinonychus were among the most
intelligent.

How long did dinosaurs live?
Studying the bones and
estimating the growth rate
of these large reptiles, some
scientists have reached the
conclusion that sauropods, like
Diplodocus and Apatosaurus, could
have lived for about 200 years.
However, there is still debate
about this.

A journey in time and place
In each chapter there is a large
reconstruction of an environment
with a brief text and a series of
notes that will help you focus on
particularly important moments in
the planet's history.

Chapter 1

The young Earth

The history of the Sun, the Earth, and the other planets and satellites in the solar system began about 5 billion years ago. At that time, exploding stars produced an enormous cloud of gas and interstellar dust in space. This primordial cloud, or nebula, consisted of hydrogen (70%), helium (27%), and heavy elements such as lead and gold (the remaining 3%). The immense span of time stretching from these early beginnings to the present day has been divided by geologists into eons, eras, periods, and epochs.

From dust to life
A shock wave generated about 5 billion years ago by an exploding star probably caused condensation of the nebula of gas and dust from which the Sun, and the disk of matter revolving around it, formed.

The Earth and the solar system
The Earth is the third planet from the Sun and is at just the right distance to make life possible. The other eight planets in the solar system are either too close or too far away from the Sun to sustain the conditions necessary for generating living organisms.

A red-hot sphere
About 4 billion years ago the Earth was a red-hot sphere. It was heated by its inner core and was constantly bombarded by comets and meteorites.

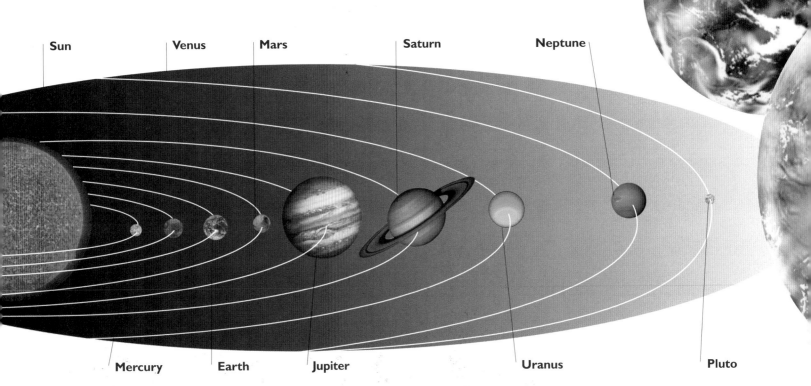

Sun   Venus   Mars   Saturn   Neptune

Mercury   Earth   Jupiter   Uranus   Pluto

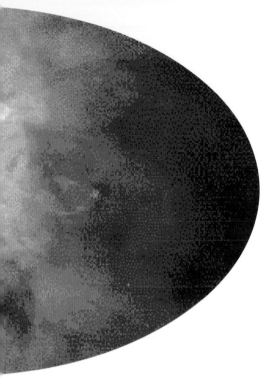

Doubts about the Earth's origins
The scientific community is not in complete agreement about the amount of time it took for the Earth and other planets to form from the primordial nebula. Obviously, no one was able to observe the solar system as it formed, nor is it possible, at least at the moment, to observe the planets of other systems. Therefore, everything we know comes from statistics based on stars that are similar, though not absolutely identical, to the Sun.

Formation of the crust
Between 4 and 3.8 billion years ago, the magma that had poured out from the core of the Earth cooled to form a primitive crust.

First forms of life
After the formation of the oceans and the primordial atmosphere, the first forms of life appeared about 3.9 billion years ago.

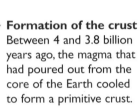

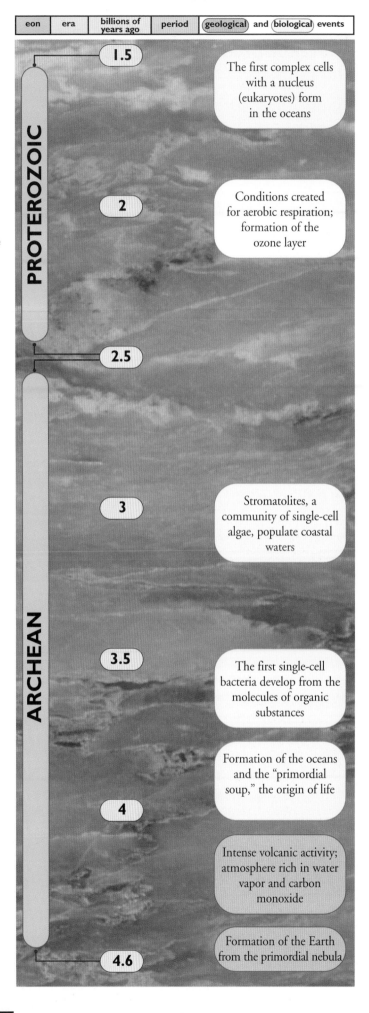

eon	era	billions of years ago	period	geological and biological events
PROTEROZOIC		1.5		The first complex cells with a nucleus (eukaryotes) form in the oceans
		2		Conditions created for aerobic respiration; formation of the ozone layer
		2.5		
ARCHEAN		3		Stromatolites, a community of single-cell algae, populate coastal waters
		3.5		The first single-cell bacteria develop from the molecules of organic substances
				Formation of the oceans and the "primordial soup," the origin of life
		4		Intense volcanic activity; atmosphere rich in water vapor and carbon monoxide
		4.6		Formation of the Earth from the primordial nebula

The structure of the Earth and the terrestrial crust

The Earth has undergone enormous changes in its history. However, thanks chiefly to the study of rocks, we can deduce a lot about the early phases of its life as well as what it is like today. The main layers making up the structure of the Earth are the core, the mantle, and the crust. To understand the chemical and physical differences among them, it has been necessary to rely on indirect evidence. The most important information has come from studies on the propagation of seismic waves caused by earthquakes. By studying how the speed of waves varies as they travel through the Earth, scientists can work out the properties of the material these waves meet on the way.

The crust

Ocean

Earth's crust is rigid and rocky. There are two types: continental crust, which forms the continents and extends beneath them for 18–24 miles (30–40 km); and oceanic crust, which is about 3–3.7 miles (5–6 km) thick. Both layers are part of the lithosphere, which also includes the upper layer of the mantle known as the asthenosphere.

Continental crust

THE FRONTIERS OF KNOWLEDGE

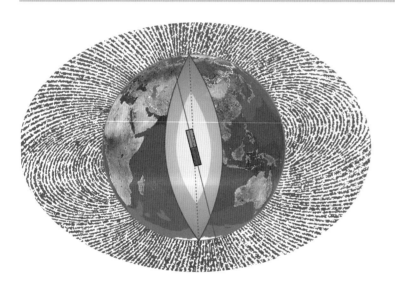

POLAR REVERSAL

Continuous currents magnetize the large masses of iron in the center of the Earth. As a result, the Earth behaves like an enormous magnet, the poles of which have been reversed a number of times over the last 3 million years. The reasons for this are not clear, nor is it known exactly what the possible consequences are, given that the last reversal took place 780,000 years ago.

The history of the Earth

The primordial dust

The enormous quantity of matter forming the primordial nebula started to contract as the result of an external storm. Over a period of 100,000–200,000 years it assumed the shape of a gassy disk wrapped in a spiral around a large, bulging center. This disk had a diameter of about 6 billion miles and was hundreds of millions of miles thick. With time the nucleus of the nebula continued to contract, becoming denser and hotter; finally the temperature and pressure became so high that the hydrogen nuclei fused with each other, generating helium nuclei.

These reactions unleashed an enormous quantity of energy that "ignited" the Sun. It still shines today, thanks to nuclear reactions taking place in its center. The Earth and other planets are bits of leftover matter that remained in orbit around the growing Sun.

Gases located far from the Sun cooled and solidified into dust and ice particles. Although these fragments were tiny, they collided with each other and aggregated to form a mass of larger bodies called planetesimals. Over a period that probably lasted tens of millions of years, further collisions of these lumps of matter led to the formation of larger bodies called protoplanets. ▶▶

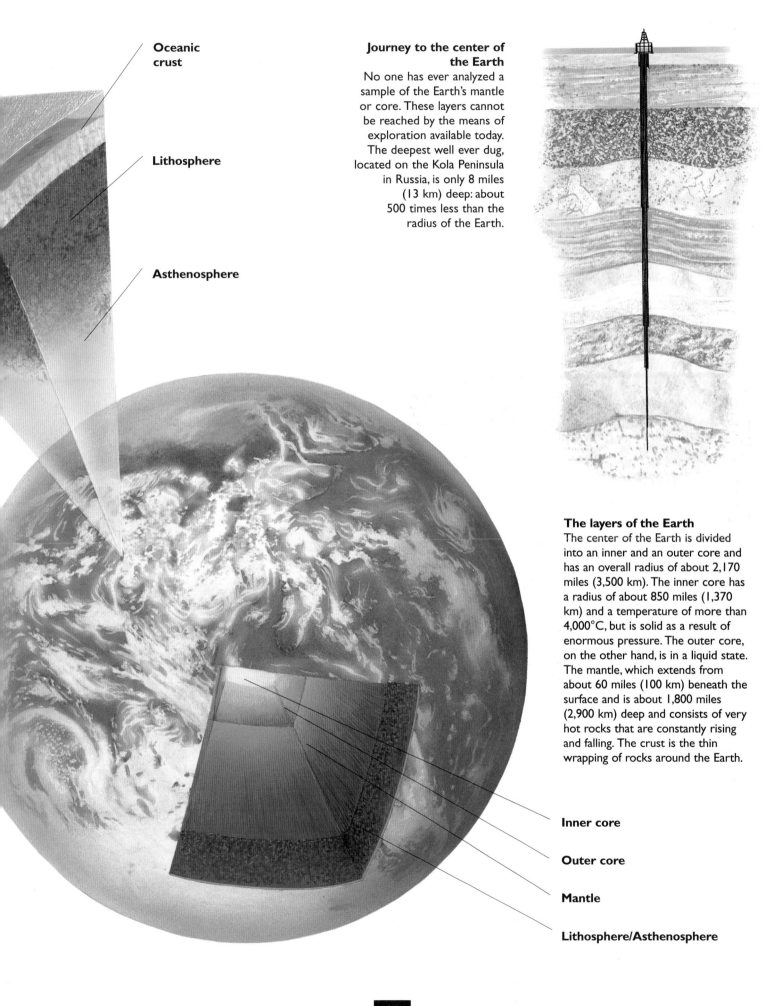

Oceanic crust

Lithosphere

Asthenosphere

Journey to the center of the Earth
No one has ever analyzed a sample of the Earth's mantle or core. These layers cannot be reached by the means of exploration available today. The deepest well ever dug, located on the Kola Peninsula in Russia, is only 8 miles (13 km) deep: about 500 times less than the radius of the Earth.

The layers of the Earth
The center of the Earth is divided into an inner and an outer core and has an overall radius of about 2,170 miles (3,500 km). The inner core has a radius of about 850 miles (1,370 km) and a temperature of more than 4,000°C, but is solid as a result of enormous pressure. The outer core, on the other hand, is in a liquid state. The mantle, which extends from about 60 miles (100 km) beneath the surface and is about 1,800 miles (2,900 km) deep and consists of very hot rocks that are constantly rising and falling. The crust is the thin wrapping of rocks around the Earth.

Inner core

Outer core

Mantle

Lithosphere/Asthenosphere

The formation of rocks

Rocks are formed from aggregates of minerals, natural substances that have a defined and fixed chemical composition. On the other hand, rocks themselves, which are our most important "documents" in reconstructing the Earth's history, are constantly undergoing change. However, very little of the Earth's early history can still be read in current rock formations, given that the oldest existing rocks, found in Greenland, date back only about 4 billion years.

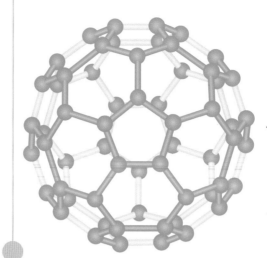

MATERIALS OF THE FUTURE

Certain pressure and temperature conditions can sometimes lead to the formation of crystals with unique and unusual properties. One of these is fullerene. In its best-known form, it consists of a 60-atom molecule resembling a soccer ball. Fullerene is a crystalline form of carbon, like diamond and graphite, and although it was not discovered until 1985, it is certain to become an important material in future technology.

Calcite

The rock cycle

The various types of rocks can be transformed from one type into another. An igneous rock that comes to the surface may crumble due to erosion by atmospheric agents. Over time, fragments of this rock may then combine with those from other sources to form a sedimentary rock. In turn, if this sedimentary rock is subjected to strong compression and high temperatures, it will be transformed into a metamorphic rock. All three types of rock may even return to a fluid state inside the mantle.

Solidification

Sodium chloride

Granite

Granite is one of the most common intrusive rocks (5%–10% of the Earth's surface). Igneous rocks that remain trapped underground are called intrusive, whereas those that reach the surface are called volcanic.

Erosion

Igneous rocks

The structure of minerals

In minerals, atoms and molecules are almost always found in regular shapes (cubes, prisms, octahedrons) called crystals. These are arranged in a regularly repeating structure, a crystalline grid, which remains constant for each mineral. The faces of crystals may form different angles in relation to the horizontal plane, as in the case of sodium chloride and calcite.

Sediments

The history of the Earth

One protoplanet was the Earth, which, like the other planets, came into being about 4.6 billion years ago. Its development was extremely violent. There was still a lot of detritus in the young solar system, and for more than 600 million years the Earth was bombarded by meteorites.

The iron core

Up to 4 billion years ago, the Earth's landscape—formed by magma and incandescent gases—must have been hellish. The enormous amount of heat generated by impacting meteorites compounded the heat radiated from elements such as uranium. Because of the increasingly high temperature, many of the materials on the surface of the primordial Earth melted.

Iron was one of the first elements to become liquid. Small wells of molten iron formed, which soon joined together into large masses. As these were heavier than other surrounding materials, they fell toward the center of the Earth, pushed by the force of gravity. In the space of a few dozen million years a core formed, similar to the current one, and the planet began to turn into a body with a precisely differentiated structure.

While the Earth separated into its various layers, the surface began to cool; this led to the formation of a very thin crust on which numerous, highly active volcanoes appeared.

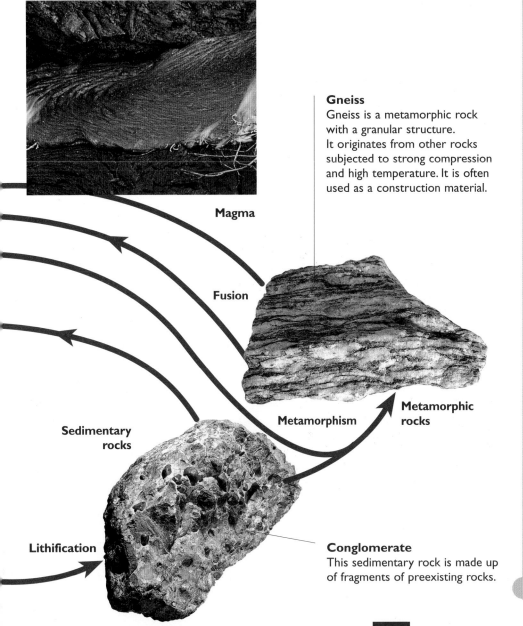

Magma

Gneiss
Gneiss is a metamorphic rock with a granular structure. It originates from other rocks subjected to strong compression and high temperature. It is often used as a construction material.

Fusion

Sedimentary rocks

Metamorphism

Metamorphic rocks

Lithification

Conglomerate
This sedimentary rock is made up of fragments of preexisting rocks.

DIAMONDS IN LEGEND

Diamonds have been called stars that have fallen to Earth and described as the tears of the gods. For the ancient Greeks, diamonds came directly from the sky and were a divine gift. There are many legends around the world about the origin of these precious stones, which consist of pure carbon. According to one myth, there was a valley full of diamonds in Asia. It was virtually unreachable, guarded from the air by ferocious predatory birds and on the ground by poisonous snakes.

The landscape
of primordial Earth

*Between 4 and 3.8 billion years ago the Earth continued
to be struck by meteorites, even though the most intense period
of bombardment was over. The planet was cooling down.
The lava erupting from volcanoes added new material to the surface
crust, which solidified and became thicker. The ocean surfaces and
large lakes shone with strange reflections caused by oily spots made
up of methane molecules. It was in these waters that the very first
forms of life began to evolve.*

A blazing hot "atmosphere"
At sunset the sky became an intense fiery
red. The colors were stronger than they are
today because the primordial atmosphere
contained a lot of dust and virtually no
oxygen.

Messengers of the past
Of the various types of meteorites that hit the surface of the planet (the process still continues
today), some have remained virtually unchanged since they formed about 4.6 billion years ago.
They supply us with crucial information about how the solar system developed, as well as the
original material that aggregated to form the Earth.

A sea of volcanoes
In this phase of the Earth's history, there were a remarkable number of volcanoes. The landscape was characterized by vapors, lapilli, and lava constantly erupting from the depths of the planet.

Volcanoes and eruptions

The extremely hot magma, or molten rock, found deep inside the Earth, is pushed up by strong pressures and comes to the surface through volcanoes.

There are two main categories of volcanoes, explosive and effusive, depending on the type of lava emitted. The lava of effusive volcanoes is hotter and more fluid, and the eruptions are nonviolent. In explosive volcanoes the magma welling to the surface is cooler and more viscous; as a result, it moves with greater difficulty and tends to obstruct the opening, creating a plug. Eruptions are very violent because they occur only when the passage to the surface is suddenly unblocked.

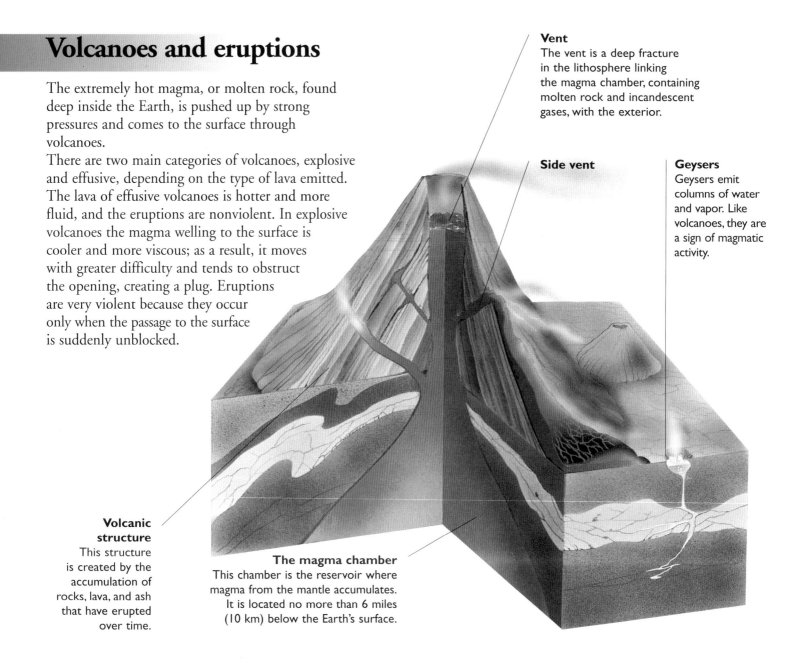

Vent
The vent is a deep fracture in the lithosphere linking the magma chamber, containing molten rock and incandescent gases, with the exterior.

Side vent

Geysers
Geysers emit columns of water and vapor. Like volcanoes, they are a sign of magmatic activity.

Volcanic structure
This structure is created by the accumulation of rocks, lava, and ash that have erupted over time.

The magma chamber
This chamber is the reservoir where magma from the mantle accumulates. It is located no more than 6 miles (10 km) below the Earth's surface.

The history of the Earth

The formation of the atmosphere and the oceans

Volcanoes provided a passage to the surface for volatile compounds. These gases from inside the Earth, together with those contained in meteorites arriving from space, formed the primordial atmosphere. This consisted mainly of ammonia, methane, water, and carbon dioxide but had virtually no oxygen. As a result, the layer of ozone (a gas made up of molecules comprising three oxygen atoms) that now protects the Earth from solar radiation did not yet exist. The Earth's surface was bombarded by ultraviolet rays that would have killed any living being on land.

At a certain stage, the mix that formed the primordial atmosphere began to condense and clouds appeared. The first oceans originated between 4 and 3.8 billion years ago, the result of millions of years of rainfall. And somewhere, in the midst of eruptions and storms, sulfur and ammonia vapors, an absolutely extraordinary phenomenon occurred. A few drops of liquid began to do something that no liquid or chemical substance had ever done before   they multiplied and replicated themselves in almost identical copies. These drops of liquid, enclosed by a membrane, were the earliest living creatures. But how were they born and how did they function? ▶▶

THE ERUPTION OF THE TAMBORA VOLCANO

The eruption of the Tambora volcano in Indonesia in 1815 is regarded as having been one of the most devastating in recent history. More than 10,000 people died in the space of just a few hours. Another 80,000 perished as a result of crop losses.

The climatic effects resulting from the darkening of the sky were felt all over the world for more than a year. In England the average temperature fell by at least 2°C, and it is no coincidence that 1816 was remembered as the "year with no summer."

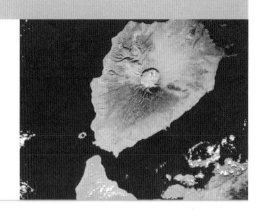

The formation of the atmosphere

In the early phases of the history of the Earth, gases from beneath the crust escaped through volcanoes (1). Clouds formed, and there began to be rainfall (2). Thanks to the rain, the water contained in meteorites, and water vapor trapped in the Earth and emitted by volcanoes, primordial oceans formed (3).

THE FRONTIERS OF KNOWLEDGE

(1)

(2)

(3)

And finally ... oxygen

The volcanic gases that gave rise to the primordial atmosphere existed for hundreds of millions of years before the appearance of oxygen. This element was produced by the first forms of aquatic life (4).

TRICKY PREDICTIONS

In order to predict whether or not a volcano is going to erupt, experts study the fracturing of surrounding rocks, the seismic activity, and the gases emitted. However, scientists have not yet come up with a really effective means of predicting eruptions. Many populations living near volcanoes still rely on nonscientific methods, for instance, observing the behavior of animals, especially fish and birds, which become strangely agitated when a lava eruption is imminent.

(4)

The first living organisms

There are many theories about the first stages of life on Earth and how they came about. No one yet knows exactly what happened. The only thing that is certain is that somewhere on primordial Earth, about 3.9 billion years ago, there appeared some small, rounded structures containing proteins and nucleic acids. They interacted through a complex chain of chemical reactions that enabled the structures to reproduce. This was the beginning of life on Earth.

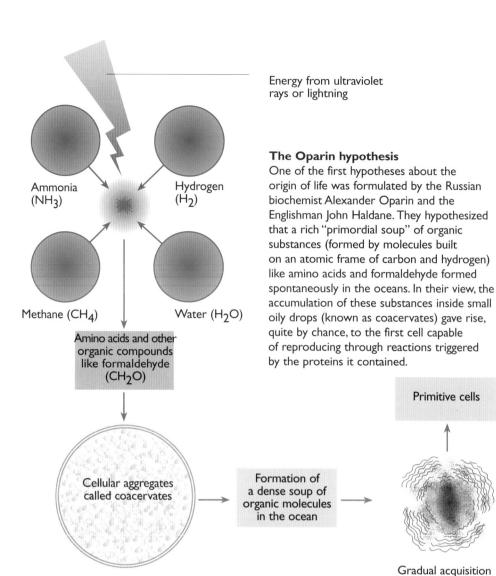

Energy from ultraviolet rays or lightning

Ammonia (NH$_3$)

Hydrogen (H$_2$)

Methane (CH$_4$)

Water (H$_2$O)

Amino acids and other organic compounds like formaldehyde (CH$_2$O)

Cellular aggregates called coacervates

Formation of a dense soup of organic molecules in the ocean

Primitive cells

Gradual acquisition of the chemical properties of the cell

The Oparin hypothesis

One of the first hypotheses about the origin of life was formulated by the Russian biochemist Alexander Oparin and the Englishman John Haldane. They hypothesized that a rich "primordial soup" of organic substances (formed by molecules built on an atomic frame of carbon and hydrogen) like amino acids and formaldehyde formed spontaneously in the oceans. In their view, the accumulation of these substances inside small oily drops (known as coacervates) gave rise, quite by chance, to the first cell capable of reproducing through reactions triggered by the proteins it contained.

THE FRONTIERS OF KNOWLEDGE

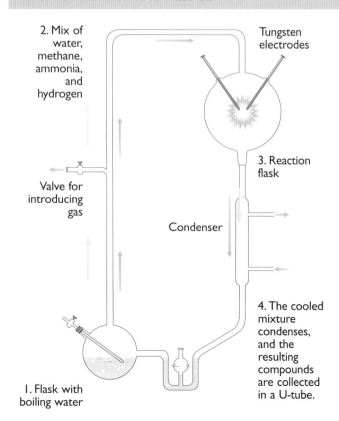

2. Mix of water, methane, ammonia, and hydrogen

Tungsten electrodes

Valve for introducing gas

Condenser

3. Reaction flask

4. The cooled mixture condenses, and the resulting compounds are collected in a U-tube.

1. Flask with boiling water

MILLER'S EXPERIMENT

In 1953, the biochemist Stanley Miller produced big sparks (similar to flashes of lightning) in a flask containing the gases presumed to have formed the atmosphere of primordial Earth. A few days later he found a brown liquid in the flask. To the amazement of scientists, it contained a number of amino acids, the basic building blocks of proteins. We now know that the primordial atmosphere was not composed as Miller thought it was, but the fact remains that organic molecules can form spontaneously from inorganic substances in an oxygen-free atmosphere.

Panspermia

Some people (like the late Fred Hoyle, an astrophysicist) believe life did not originate on Earth but in certain regions of outer space rich in organic molecules and warm gases, and that life arrived on Earth in comets or meteorites. The biologist Francis Crick, who was awarded a Nobel prize for discovering the structure of DNA, has even suggested that the earliest microorganisms might have come to Earth on spacecraft sent by other civilizations to "sow" life in the universe. These are panspermia or "universal seed" hypotheses.

The world of RNA

A Nobel prize winner for chemistry, Tom Cech, discovered that RNA molecules, which are found in all living cells, are capable of replicating in certain conditions in association with a particular enzyme. Some experts have therefore hypothesized that the predecessors of all living beings might have been various simple RNA molecules that replicated. After millions of years, and having come in contact with protein complexes, RNA copies formed the first complete living cells, each of which was equipped with a single RNA molecule that replicated itself.

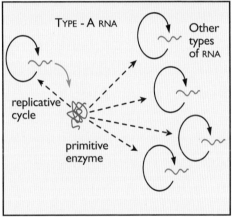

In the presence of a certain enzyme, various types of RNA reproduce themselves and spread in the environment.

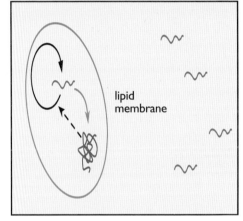

Protected from the external environment, a single type of RNA can reproduce itself inside a membrane, giving rise to a primitive cell with its own genetic structure.

The history of the Earth

The birth of life

We now know a good deal about the basic mechanisms underlying the functioning of each living being. All organisms consist of one or more cells, which are different in shape and size but which all share the ability to reproduce. All cells function by means of chemical reactions based on two main categories of substances, proteins and nucleic acids.

Proteins are chains formed by hundreds of thousands of molecules called amino acids. They are produced by the organism and function as construction blocks for important parts of the cell; they also serve as substances for transporting other useful molecules, as well as for controlling and regulating chemical reactions indispensable for survival, such as breathing, the digestion of food, photosynthesis, and so forth. Nucleic acids (DNA and RNA), on the other hand, are molecules formed by long chains of smaller molecules called nitrogenous bases. Deoxyribonucleic acid (DNA) is the "genetic material" of the organism. It includes all the characteristics inherited from our parents and contains, on segments called genes, the information needed to form amino acids and produce the proteins required by the organism. ▶▶

DNA, RNA, proteins, and the genetic code

How did the first organisms succeed in replicating themselves so exactly? The explanation lies in the mechanisms governing cell functioning, which are based on the characteristics of two fundamental classes of molecules: proteins, which form many parts of the cell and regulate its functioning, and nucleic acids, which codify and regulate the production of proteins.

Proteins

A protein is a sometimes very long chain of amino acids wound into a complex three-dimensional structure. This structure contains linear and spiral-shaped segments, respectively called beta-sheets and alpha-helixes. The properties of a protein depend largely on its three-dimensional form.

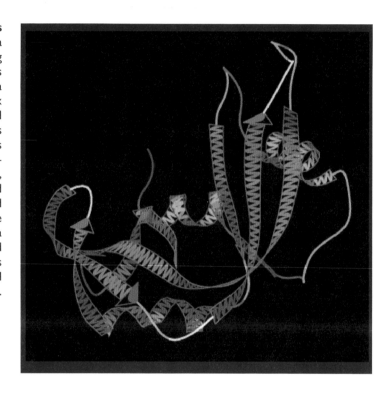

DNA

The DNA molecule, coiled up inside a cell, occupies a millionth of a yard. However, if we could unravel the DNA molecule of a human cell, consisting of a sequence of more than 3 billion nitrogenous bases, into a straight line, it would be a couple of yards long. There are four different nitrogenous bases: adenine, thymine, guanine, and cytosine. For each sequence of three nitrogenous bases, there is, according to the genetic code, 1 of 20 types of amino acids used for the synthesis of proteins.

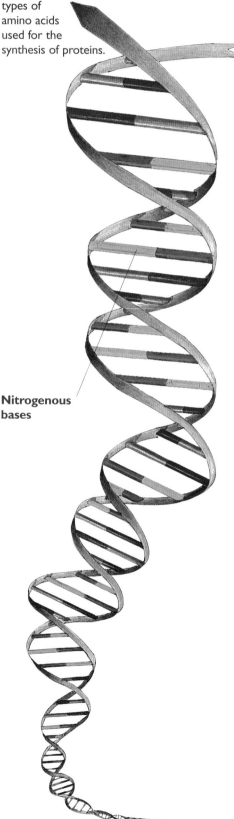

Nitrogenous bases

STORIES AND PIONEERS OF SCIENCE

THE CONTRIBUTION OF ROSALIND FRANKLIN

James Watson, Francis Crick, and Maurice Wilkins were awarded a Nobel prize for their discovery of DNA's double-helix structure in 1953. However, an English biophysicist named Rosalind Franklin, as brilliant as she was unfortunate, made a crucial contribution. Using a technique called x-ray crystallography, Franklin discovered that the structure carrying the DNA molecule is a strip of sugars and phosphates. She was the first to understand that the molecule is spiral-shaped. Watson and Crick used her data but never acknowledged her contribution. She died of cancer in 1958, at the age of 37.

The instructions for building proteins are 'written' in a genetic code, in which the sequence of nitrogenous bases on a gene has a corresponding sequence of amino acids.

Ribonucleic acid (RNA) copies and transfers the information contained in DNA, using it to translate the sequences of nitrogenous bases into sequences of amino acids. Nucleic acids are also capable, with the help of proteins, of replicating and directing duplication of the entire cell.

There are many theories about how the first organisms formed. What is certain is that living beings very similar to present-day bacteria existed on Earth between 3.9 and 3.8 billion years ago and that they almost certainly lived underwater, which protected them from ultraviolet rays. But in a world with no plants, fungi, or animals, what did they eat?

What's for dinner?

All organisms need energy and matter in order to live. In other words, they need to feed off something. The first microorganisms obtained what they needed from hydrogen, sulfur, and certain metals; they drew energy from the heat of the environment. Subsequently, some organisms began to engulf and digest nearby beings. The first predators had come into being. ▸▸

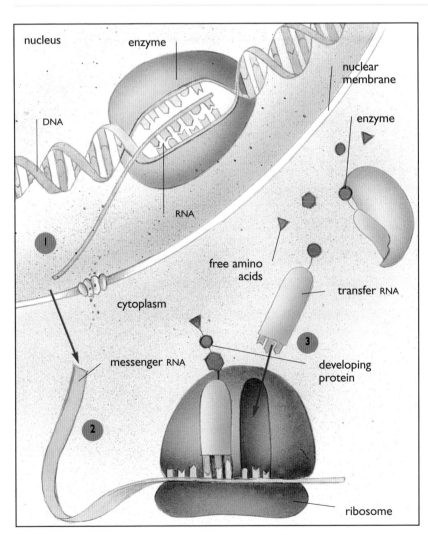

Protein synthesis
DNA contains all the information a cell needs to synthesize proteins. This is how synthesis comes about:
1) Some enzymes (proteins that favor certain chemical processes) open the double helix of DNA at the point of the segment (gene) where the information required to synthesize a particular protein is recorded. This is copied by an RNA molecule called a messenger.
2) The messenger RNA transports the information to a structure called the ribosome, which acts as a protein assembly line.
3) Another type of RNA, known as transfer RNA, picks up amino acids roaming freely in the cell and takes them to the ribosome, where they are assembled, according to the sequence codified on the messenger RNA, to form the protein.

HOW MANY GENES ARE THERE?

It was once thought that each gene encoded just one protein and that human DNA consequently contained hundreds of thousands of genes. In actual fact, thanks to a series of mechanisms, a gene can be involved in the synthesis of various proteins. Thanks to the Human Genome Project, since 2001 we have known our DNA sequence with considerable precision. There are about a 100,000 human genes, not many more than the quantity possessed by the drosophila, a fly commonly studied in research! The complexity of an organism therefore depends not so much on the number of genes as on the relations among them. Most of these have yet to be discovered.

Autotrophs and heterotrophs

As the number and variety of organisms present on Earth grew, the problem of obtaining food and energy became more pressing. Some organisms, known as autotrophs ("that feed by themselves"), found a way of synthesizing the substances they needed internally. Heterotrophs ("that feed off others") opted for another strategy: They ate other living organisms.

STORIES AND PIONEERS OF SCIENCE

THE WORLD IN A DROP OF WATER

The existence of microorganisms remained undiscovered until the seventeenth century. A Dutchman, Antony van Leeuwenhoek (1632–1723), managed to grind lenses with incredible precision and built more than 250 microscopes, some of which were capable of a magnification of 300X. Using these instruments, he noted that a drop of stagnant water contained a large community of "tiny animals" of all shapes and sizes. He was the first person to identify protozoa and bacteria, thereby giving rise to the science of microbiology.

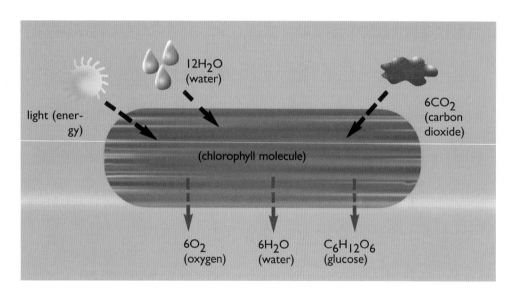

12H_2O (water)

light (energy)

6CO_2 (carbon dioxide)

(chlorophyll molecule)

6O_2 (oxygen)

6H_2O (water)

$C_6H_{12}O_6$ (glucose)

Photosynthesis

The most well-known autotroph organisms are those capable of chlorophyllous photosynthesis, such as plants and cyanobacteria. The basic units are simple and extremely common: carbon dioxide and water molecules. These compounds are made to interact and are broken down. Their atoms are then reassembled to form sugar (glucose), oxygen, and water molecules. This reaction requires energy, which is provided by solar rays.
Although the chlorophyll molecule does not take an active part in photosynthesis, it makes the reaction possible by absorbing solar energy and distributing it to other molecules.

The history of the Earth

Some cells, rather than extracting energy from the heat of the Earth or from food, obtain it from sunlight. To do so, some of them made use of a new chemical reaction that was to change the history of the planet: They transformed water and carbon dioxide into glucose and oxygen. These beings were cyanobacteria, and they had invented photosynthesis.
There are fossil traces of cyanobacteria in rocks in Australia and South Africa that are 3.5 billion years old, and they still exist today all over the planet. At the time they formed immense colonies on sea beds, in layers called stromatolites. These colonies developed into great rocky barriers.

Oxygen: vital or lethal?

Cyanobacteria multiplied all over the planet and polluted the atmosphere with the waste product of photosynthesis: oxygen. Today oxygen is crucial for the survival of the majority of living beings. But it is a very active gas that oxidizes many substances, attacking and modifying them radically. For primordial organisms it was a deadly poison.
About 2.2 billion years ago, the concentration of oxygen in the atmosphere started to rise dramatically. In the space of just a few hundred million years, it rose from 1% to 20% of the atmosphere. It was the first global pollution crisis caused by living beings. ▶▶

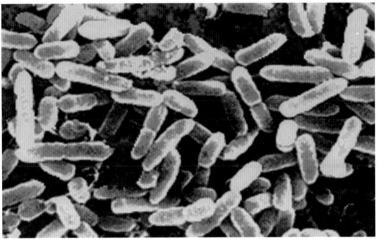

"DIGESTING" OIL

In the last 20 years, genetic engineering has been used to develop numerous strains of bacteria capable of breaking down pollutants. One of the first of these was a bacterium of the genus Pseudomonas, *created by the American scientist Ananda Chakrabarty in the 1970s.*

This bacterium is capable of partially "digesting" oil. It was also the first living being to be patented (in 1981). There is a vigorous debate about the benefits and risks of releasing such microorganisms into the environment and whether living organisms should be patented.

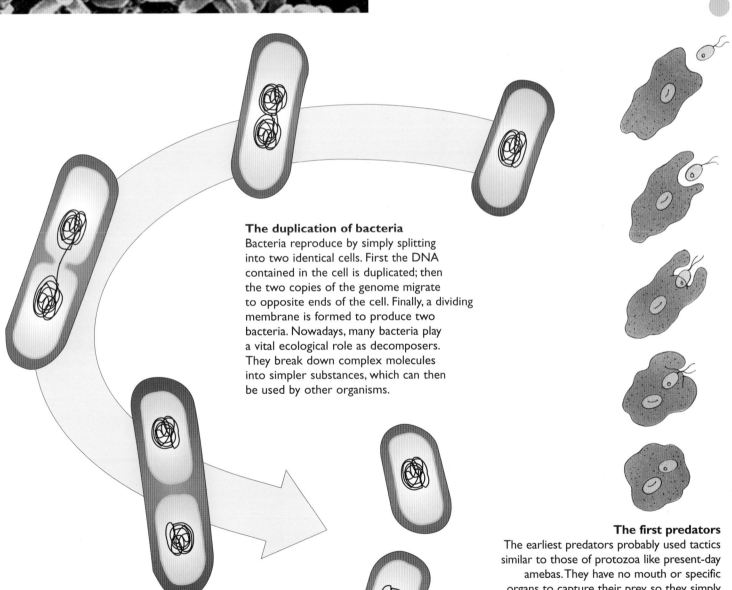

The duplication of bacteria
Bacteria reproduce by simply splitting into two identical cells. First the DNA contained in the cell is duplicated; then the two copies of the genome migrate to opposite ends of the cell. Finally, a dividing membrane is formed to produce two bacteria. Nowadays, many bacteria play a vital ecological role as decomposers. They break down complex molecules into simpler substances, which can then be used by other organisms.

The first predators
The earliest predators probably used tactics similar to those of protozoa like present-day amebas. They have no mouth or specific organs to capture their prey, so they simply modify their form in order to engulf it. This is known as phagocytosis. The prey is then broken down by particular proteins called digestive enzymes; finally, the waste materials are expelled.

Present-day cells

Eukaryotic cells, like the ones that make up our bodies and those of all higher animals and plants, were an extraordinary evolutionary development. The cell became a microscopic "factory" where different functions were carried out in different compartments by means of specialized organelles coordinated and regulated by a complex network of chemical reactions and messages.

But how did the earliest eukaryotic cells develop? Were they possibly due to a chance alliance between different microorganisms?

Prokaryotic cells
Prokaryotic cells, like those of bacteria, have a very simple internal structure; the DNA and ribosomes move around freely inside the cell. Some bacteria have cilia on the external membrane, which are useful for attaching onto other objects, or mobile flagella enabling locomotion.

DNA

Ribosomes

Cilia

Flagella

The Margulis hypothesis
According to the biologist Lynn Margulis, the first eukaryotic cells may have formed as a result of symbiosis between prokaryotes, that is to say, a mutually beneficial cohabitation between different bacteria.

The flagella of current-day cells might originally have been threadlike bacteria similar to present-day spirochetes.

Basic prokaryote organism.

Formation of the first eukaryotic organism with a flagellum.

Bacteria capable of using oxygen to obtain energy may have entered prokaryotic cells as prey or parasites and then evolved into mitochondria.

Evolution of the flagellate eukaryote, giving rise to the branch of animals.

Cyanobacteria, which are capable of carrying out photosynthesis, may have been the ancestors of chloroplasts, thereby giving rise to the branch of plants.

The history of the Earth

The majority of living organisms at the time were faced with a dramatic situation. Those that did not live hidden in rocks or in the ocean depths had to find a way to make oxygen harmless. They evolved a way of "burning" it before it could attack the insides of cells. They made it react with glucose to produce water and carbon dioxide. Known today as cellular respiration, this chemical reaction had the added advantage of providing useful energy for the functioning of the cell.

Burning glucose was a new way of obtaining energy. In this way, microscopic cyanobacteria laid the foundations for the evolution of all complex forms of life; thanks to oxygen, respiration became possible.

Later oxygen was also responsible for formation of the protective ozone layer, which would enable life forms to emerge from the water.

In the meantime, eukaryotes appeared between 1.8 and 1.5 billion years ago. These organisms still had only one cell but they were much more complex than bacteria and cyanobacteria.

The birth of eukaryotic organisms was the first step in an extraordinary evolutionary process on Earth. However, a lot more time would elapse before the world witnessed the incomparable spectacle of the evolution of thousands of different species.

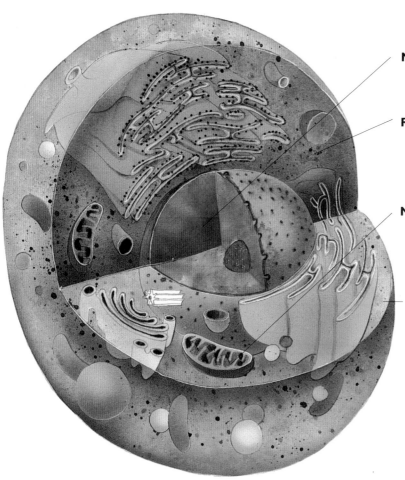

Nucleus

Ribosomes

Mitochondrion

Plasmatic membrane

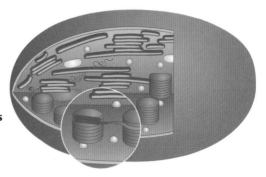

Chloroplasts

Photosynthesis takes place in chloroplasts, which are found, for instance, in all plant cells. Chlorophyll is contained in microscopic disk-shaped structures called thylakoids. These are stacked on top of each other and embedded in a supporting structure called a stroma.

Eukaryotic cells

A large part of the DNA in eukaryotes is protected inside a nucleus and organized in structures called chromosomes. In the cytoplasm, structures called microtubules and microfilaments provide a support matrix for the cell. Numerous organelles, or differentiated compartments, carry out various vital cell functions: producing energy, synthesizing molecules, storing nutrients, and so on.

Mitochondria

Mitochondria are organelles responsible for cellular respiration. Glucose is "burned" with oxygen to produce water, carbon dioxide, and energy, which the cell uses for its own metabolism. Cells requiring large quantities of energy (muscle cells, for example) may contain thousands of mitochondria.

THE FRONTIERS OF KNOWLEDGE

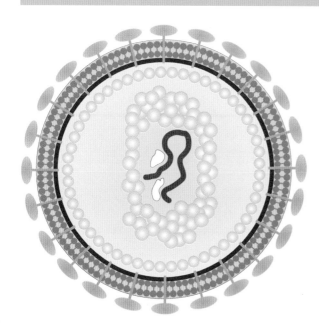

HORIZONTAL GENETIC TRANSFER

The history of the complex interaction between organisms is fascinating but still relatively unknown. We now know that many horizontal gene transfers may have taken place in our evolutionary history, in other words, not between parents and offspring but between different organisms.

For example, some viruses are capable of permanently transferring part of their DNA to the organisms they infect. Many segments deriving from viruses have been found in human DNA.

Chapter 2
The explosion of life

Toward the end of the Proterozoic, between 850 and 600 million years ago, the continents were quite similar in size to those that exist today. In fact the land masses had already begun to collide and separate. Their relative positions were very different compared to now, though it is not certain what they were.

In the meantime another decisive step was about to take place in the development of life: the establishment of multicellular organisms.

But if the first cells present on Earth always replicated themselves identically, how could this possibly come about?

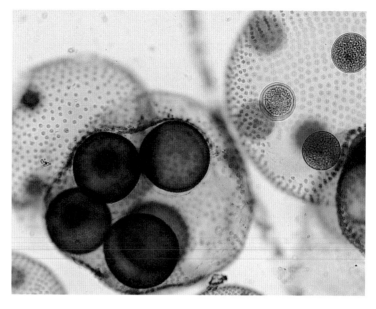

The earliest multicellular organisms
Volvox is a present-day organism that gives us an idea of how the earliest multicellular beings probably functioned. It comprises a colony of several tens of thousands of identical single-cell algae.
Incapable of surviving on their own, they group together in a spherical structure and share tasks.

The Ediacara fauna
Wonderfully preserved fossil remains in the Ediacara Hills in Australia reveal forms of life that are incredibly diverse from those that exist today. Only jellyfish—which date back hundreds of millions of years and are among the earliest multicellular organisms in the oceans—can still be observed today in seas all over the planet.

Charnia
This mysterious organism, which grew up to 3 feet in length, resembled a leaf or a bird's feather and probably lived anchored to the sea bed. Similar organisms can be found in the Pacific Ocean today. They are called sea pens and are distant relatives of corals.

Arkarua adami
According to some experts, this creature was one of the earliest echinoderms, the group that also includes present-day sea urchins.

The origin of skeletal structures

Skeletal structures such as the shell and exoskeleton originated in a salt-rich marine environment. In fact, they were formed by minerals deposited on a matrix of collagen, the most important and most commonly found structural protein in the animal kingdom. The oldest known skeletal remains are microscopic button-shaped structures first discovered in rocks in Siberia, which were probably incorporated within the bodies of ancient animals.

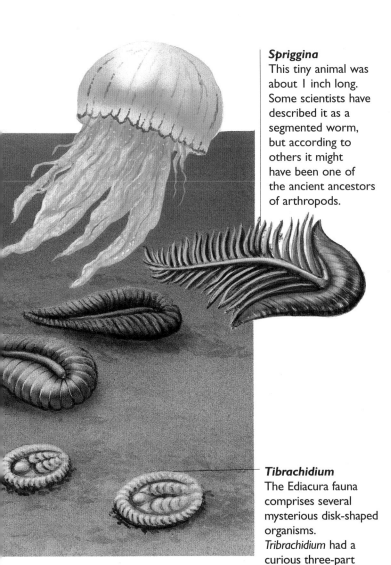

Spriggina
This tiny animal was about 1 inch long. Some scientists have described it as a segmented worm, but according to others it might have been one of the ancient ancestors of arthropods.

Tibrachidium
The Ediacura fauna comprises several mysterious disk-shaped organisms. *Tibrachidium* had a curious three-part symmetry. It is not clear whether it has living descendants.

eon	era	millions of years ago	period	geological and biological events
		245		
PHANEROZOIC	PALEOZOIC		Permian	80% of living species become extinct
				Land masses join together into the Pangaea supercontinent
		286		
			Carboniferous	Appearance of reptiles
				Appearance of amphibians; large forests cover dry land
		360		
			Devonian	North America, Greenland, and Scotland join onto Europe
				Appearance of fish
		408		
			Silurian	
		438		Earliest sea vertebrates; arthropods and earliest plants colonize the Earth
			Ordovician	
		505		
			Cambrian	A large continental mass forms around the South Pole
		570		
PROTEROZOIC				Well-differentiated invertebrates populate the ocean beds; algae are the only forms of flora
		800		
		1000		

Evolution

There is no plan, goal, or predetermined path in evolution. There is no inherent tendency to gradually create more and more complex or intelligent organisms. There is simply a tendency to favor all those living forms that succeed in surviving and reproducing in a given environment. Driven by a mechanism of chance mutations in the genome, evolution's great test is natural selection.

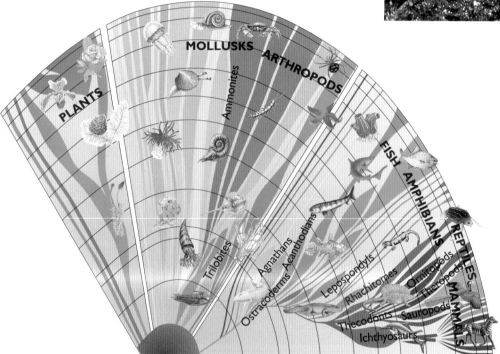

Genetic variability
The individuals of a species, even if they live in the same population and even if they have the same parents, are not generally the same. Genetic variability, resulting from chance mutations or sexual reproduction, is reflected in differing external features of organisms.

The evolution of living beings
Thanks to a subtle but unceasing process of mutation and selection of individuals from one generation to the next, increasingly differentiated species and groups of organisms appear over periods of millions of years. They all descend from a very distant common ancestor formed from a single cell.

The history of the Earth

Two motors of evolution: chance and necessity

When a cell reproduces, its DNA replicates into two theoretically identical copies. However, in the sequence of millions or billions of nitrogenous bases that make up the letters of the great book of inheritable characteristics, occasionally a bad copy is made. Chemical substances and radiation can affect certain delicate phases in the replication of the double helix and cause mutations, that is, the insertion of nitrogenous bases that are different from the original sequence.

Mutations, where not all the replicating cells produce identical daughter cells, lead to genetic variability. This variability can be very useful. Many mutations are neutral, bringing neither advantages nor disadvantages to the organism, whereas the majority of mutations that modify the form of a protein are deadly because they alter the functioning of the organism too radically. Yet some rare mutations can prove advantageous to those who have them. For example, they can make it possible to exploit surrounding resources more effectively, to use resources that no one else is using, to adapt to a sudden change in environmental conditions, or to develop a more effective defense against predators. The few organisms carrying such mutations reproduce faster or for a longer period than their nonmutant counterparts. As a result, their numbers increase rapidly in the space of just a few generations. ▶▶

Mutation ...

The pepper moth, *Biston betularia*, lives near birch trees, which have a characteristic white bark. Normally the butterfly's wings are very pale. When a mutant dark-colored butterfly is born, it has little chance of survival because it shows up against the background of the birch tree, making it easy prey for birds. However, near industrial plants soot darkens tree trunks, and selection permits the existence of darker individuals.

... and selection

Some scientists claim to have discovered that in areas where the trunks of birch trees are darkened by pollution, a population of dark-colored butterflies soon appears. If the pollution disappears, the butterflies become pale-colored again in the space of a few generations. According to this theory, individual variability is channeled by the pressure of natural selection.

THE FRONTIERS OF KNOWLEDGE

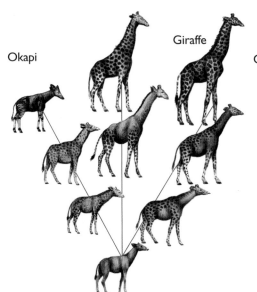

Evolutionary tree of the okapi and the giraffe according to the gradualist theory

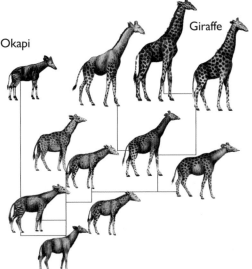

Evolutionary tree of the okapi and the giraffe according to the theory of punctuated equilibrium

EVOLUTION: GRADUALISM OR PUNCTUATED EQUILIBRIUM?

The basic mechanisms of evolutionary theory have now been amply demonstrated. Yet it is still not quite clear how the great differences that exist between living species come about. According to some scientists, the process of evolution is very slow and gradual, whereas according to others, long periods of little or no change are interrupted by sudden, drastic, macroscopic transitions toward new species.

The dance of the tectonic plates

The outer part of the Earth, the lithosphere, is not rigid and unbroken but is formed by about 20 plates, of which there are 7 main ones. These plates are in slow but constant movement in relation to each other and are a bit like rafts; they drift on the intermediate part of the mantle, the asthenosphere, which is hot and flowing. Because of the constant movement of the plates, the appearance of the Earth is constantly changing, albeit slowly. Phenomena relating to these movements are explained by the theory of plate tectonics formulated in the 1960s. This theory built on previous theories like that of continental drift, which states that only the continents, and not the entire lithosphere, are in movement.

WEGENER AND CONTINENTAL DRIFT

We owe the idea of continental drift to the German meteorologist Alfred Wegener, who expounded the theory in his book Die Entstehung der Kontinente und Ozeane (On the Origins of Continents and Oceans), *published in 1915. His theory was incomplete and heavily criticized at the time, especially by physicists; they believed that the outer part of the Earth was too rigid to enable the continents to move on the sea.*

350 million years ago
At the beginning of the Carboniferous the continents were all moving toward each other.

200 million years ago
Today's continents comprised a single, large supercontinent called Pangaea, which after several million years is thought to have broken up into two parts, Gondwana in the south and Laurasia in the north.

100 million years ago
Pangaea had broken apart. The Atlantic Ocean had almost completely separated the Americas from Europe and Asia. India formed a separate continent.

The history of the Earth

Evolution is therefore driven by chance (natural mutation, which causes variability between organisms) and necessity (the pressure of selection, which condemns to extinction any species unable to compete and reproduce efficiently). Thanks to these forces, the Earth is not inhabited by copies of the earliest organism but by continually mutating species.

Strength in union

Multicellularity probably originated when some eukaryotic cells produced by the multiplication of a single cell failed to separate but remained together, thereby exploiting a number of advantages. First of all, by becoming bigger,

organisms could protect themselves more effectively from predators. Over time some groups of cells specialized and eventually formed tissues and organs with specific functions. This union led, for instance, to the evolution of cells capable of producing poison to paralyze a prey or of developing more efficient structures for grabbing hold of it. Multicellularity also led to another important step in the history of life—the emergence of sexual reproduction.

The advantages of sexual reproduction

Some multicellular organisms developed specialized cells for reproduction. These are called gametes and are of two types, male and female. ▸▸

Plate boundaries

This map shows the current plate boundaries. Earthquakes and volcanic activity prevalently occur along these demarcation lines. Some plates include only oceanic crust, others only continental crust. Some have both types.

Collision and separation of plates

When a denser oceanic plate collides with a less dense continental one, the former sinks beneath the latter in a process called subduction. The separation of plates, on the other hand, produces a phenomenon that mainly takes place beneath the sea: Magma wells up from the mantle to form a new sea bed. The material seeps out from ocean ridges, complex systems of fractures in the oceanic crust that are sometimes thousands of miles long.

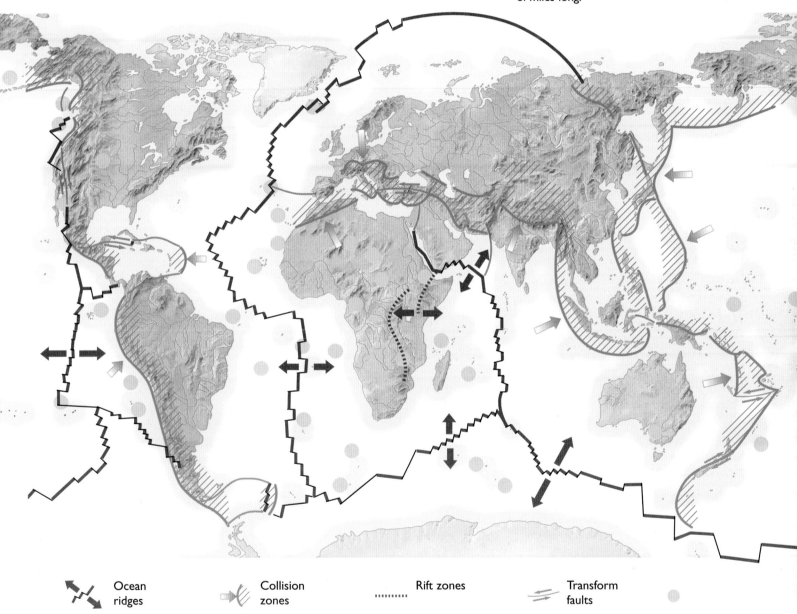

Ocean ridges	Collision zones	Rift zones	Transform faults

Plate movements

The arrows indicate possible movements of the plates, which may collide, slide past each other, or separate. The speed of movement varies, but on average is a few inches a year.

Transform faults

Faults are long, vertical fractures along which plates slide laterally against each other. This motion, known as transform or transcurrent motion, neither consumes nor produces crust.

Rivers, lakes, mountains

Mountain chains are formed when two plates collide with each other. The Earth's deepest lakes, on the other hand, are the result of water filling cracks in the Earth's crust created by movement of the lithosphere. Other lakes are formed by melting glaciers or by the obstruction of a watercourse. The formation of rivers is unrelated to plate movements; they are usually fed by water that has accumulated in natural cavities in the terrain.

Lake Tanganyika
Lake Tanganyika is one of the deepest in the world. Its maximum depth is 4,712 feet (1,450 m) and it has an elongated shape. These characteristics are typical of tectonic lakes, which generally form as a result of the sinking of the Earth's crust due to seismic and volcanic activity.

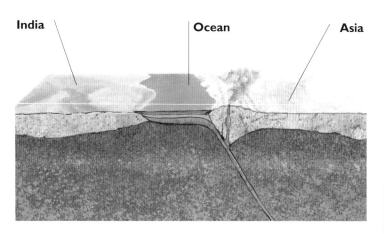

India   Ocean   Asia

The formation of the Himalayas
About 50 million years ago, the Himalayas, the Asian mountain chain that has the Earth's highest summits, still did not exist.

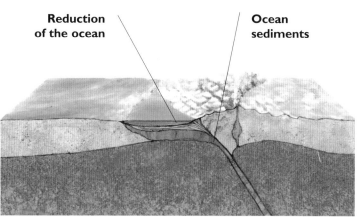

Reduction of the ocean   Ocean sediments

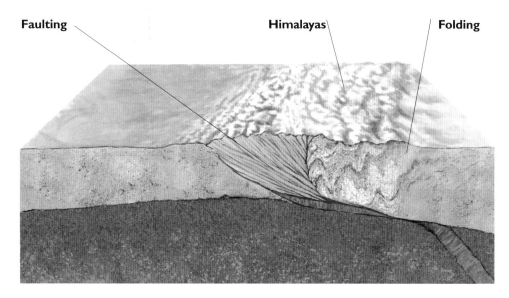

Faulting   Himalayas   Folding

An unfinished process
The ocean that separated the two continents receded and finally disappeared. Meantime the sediments of the seabed were thrust up to form, in the space of 30 million years, the Himalayan mountain chain. The process that pushes India northward, compressing it against Asia, is still going on today.

In higher animals male gametes are called spermatozoai, female ones are ova. Their union, called fertilization, gives rise to new organisms.

Procreation by means of two types of reproductive cells offers a big advantage over asexual reproduction. In the latter a single organism generates the daughter organism, which is genetically identical to the parent (unless there is some form of mutation). In sexual reproduction, on the other hand, individuals receive half their chromosomes from the mother and half from the father. This introduces a genetic variability that is useful in dealing with environmental changes. Thanks to sex, multicellular organisms are able to maintain the capacity to adapt to different situations and new threats.

The Cambrian explosion

The oldest ancestors of all known animals appeared about 540 million years ago during what is known as the "Cambrian explosion." This was an exceptional increase in the variety of living beings. At least 100 "models" (or phyla) of animals, more than triple the number there are today, became established, resulting in a sharp proliferation in life forms. We still do not really know why a billion years went by before this unprecedented spread of flora and fauna occurred in the silent waters of the primitive oceans. ▶▶

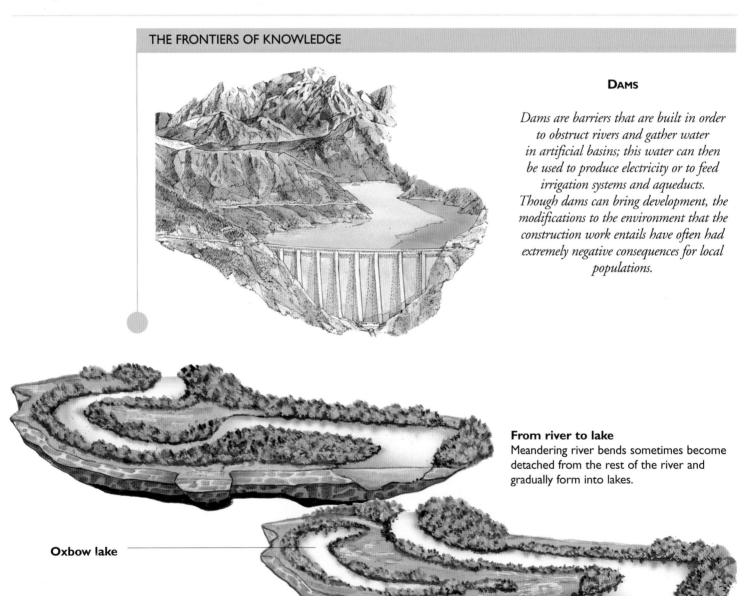

THE FRONTIERS OF KNOWLEDGE

DAMS

Dams are barriers that are built in order to obstruct rivers and gather water in artificial basins; this water can then be used to produce electricity or to feed irrigation systems and aqueducts. Though dams can bring development, the modifications to the environment that the construction work entails have often had extremely negative consequences for local populations.

From river to lake
Meandering river bends sometimes become detached from the rest of the river and gradually form into lakes.

Oxbow lake

In the waters of the Cambrian

The first animals with skeletons and hard shells appeared about 540 million years ago. These features were the result of a process known as biomineralization, which was very important for the proliferation of life. Animals with "armor" had a greater likelihood of surviving because their soft body parts were protected against attack by predators. In the meantime predators had evolved pincers and other instruments of attack. There was coevolution between prey and predator, which favored the prey with the best defense and the predator with the most developed weapons of attack. The formation of rigid structures in animals was made possible by changes in the chemical composition of the water. The oceans had in fact been enriched with minerals produced by the metabolism of organisms.

Anomalocaris
This creature was one of the most ferocious predators in the Cambrian seas. Up to a yard long, it had two large front limbs and strange toothlike platelets around the mouth.

Pikaia
Just 1 or 2 inches long, this organism may be an ancient ancestor of vertebrates. Along the axis of its body it had a strip of cells called a notochord, which was perhaps a rough, early approximation of a spinal column. Muscles became grafted onto the notochord in a pattern similar to that in fish. These made *Pikaia* capable of rapid, sinuous movement.

Marrella
Delicate, elegant, and feathery in appearance, *Marrella* was one of the most common arthropods. It varied in size from 0.1 to 0.75 inch.

Shells
Shells appeared all over the world in a very brief period of time during the Cambrian. Consisting of hard minerals, they belonged to animals that had begun to secrete a skeleton.

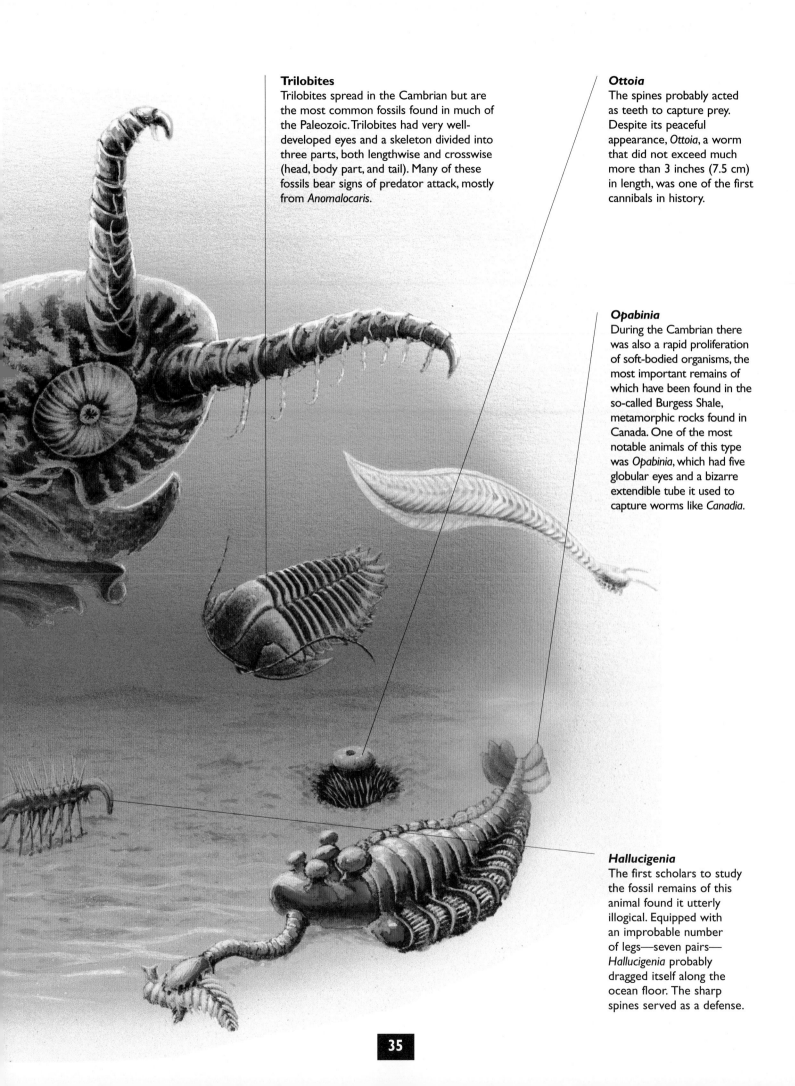

Trilobites

Trilobites spread in the Cambrian but are the most common fossils found in much of the Paleozoic. Trilobites had very well-developed eyes and a skeleton divided into three parts, both lengthwise and crosswise (head, body part, and tail). Many of these fossils bear signs of predator attack, mostly from *Anomalocaris*.

Ottoia

The spines probably acted as teeth to capture prey. Despite its peaceful appearance, *Ottoia*, a worm that did not exceed much more than 3 inches (7.5 cm) in length, was one of the first cannibals in history.

Opabinia

During the Cambrian there was also a rapid proliferation of soft-bodied organisms, the most important remains of which have been found in the so-called Burgess Shale, metamorphic rocks found in Canada. One of the most notable animals of this type was *Opabinia*, which had five globular eyes and a bizarre extendible tube it used to capture worms like *Canadia*.

Hallucigenia

The first scholars to study the fossil remains of this animal found it utterly illogical. Equipped with an improbable number of legs—seven pairs—*Hallucigenia* probably dragged itself along the ocean floor. The sharp spines served as a defense.

The primitive oceans

Sponges, jellyfish, trilobites, and all the inconspicuous creatures hidden beneath marine algae, made up the "living carpet" of primitive ocean floors. During the Ordovician and Silurian many genera of animals still with us today appeared for the first time. Swimming around amid the swarm of crustaceans, sea urchins, and mollusks enclosed in bivalve shells there were also ostracoderms, the ancestors of present-day fish. Despite the attacks of ferocious arthropods, ostracoderms differentiated into various evolutionary lines and flourished for more than fifty million years.

Subaquatic scorpions
Primitive relatives of the poisonous, hot-climate scorpions, sea scorpions were predators. They were several yards long and were equipped with powerful pincers. They had a flat body, streamlined legs, and eyes positioned on the back of the head. To protect themselves against these scorpions, many creatures developed armored shells.

Crinoids
Known as "sea lilies," the crinoids of this period were not in fact plants but echinoderms, a group of animals that included sea stars. They fed by filtering small food particles from seawater. Their skeletons consisted of hundreds of thin platelets that usually broke off after they died.

Hemicyclaspis
Hemicyclaspis was one of the cephalaspids, the first vertebrates to possess mobile appendages. They obtained food by filtering seawater. Part of the water, containing edible detritus, reached the "intestine," and the rest exited from special openings beneath the mouth.

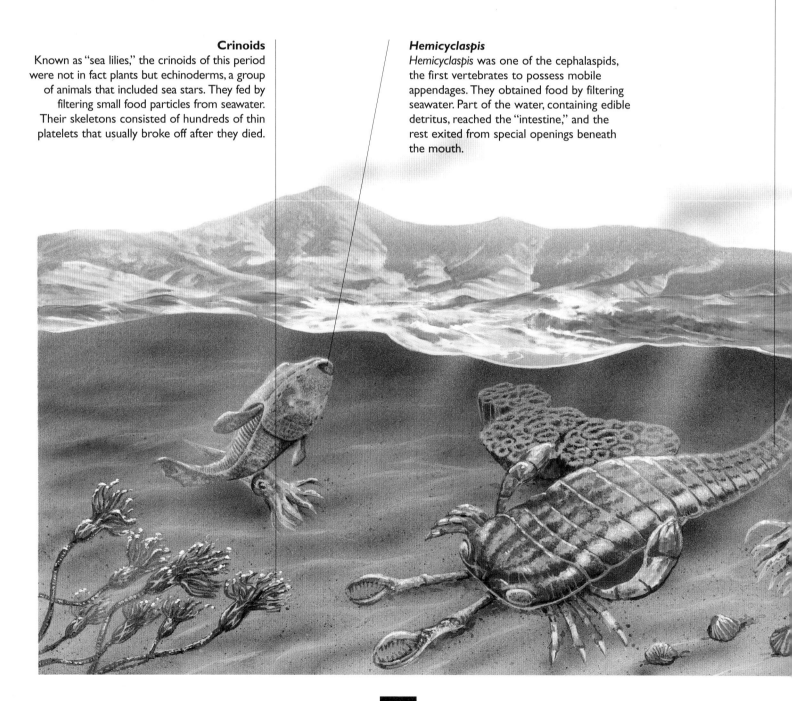

The birth of vertebrates

In the Cambrian seas, amid trilobites and other strange creatures, there was also a small ribbon-shaped organism barely 2 inches long. It did not look particularly impressive, but *Pikaia* possessed an extremely important feature. Some of its cells were arranged in a compact skeletal rod called a notochord, to which muscles were connected. One of the first living beings to possess a structure similar to a spinal column, *Pikaia* was thus the prelude to the birth of vertebrates—fish, amphibians and reptiles, mammals, and birds.

While there was an explosion of life in the waters of the primordial oceans, there was almost no trace of living beings on the continents. The land environment was vast and predator-free, but it was hard to colonize. The two major obstacles were the lack of oxygen and the damaging ultraviolet rays of the Sun, which were not shielded then, as they are today, by the protective layer of ozone in the upper atmosphere.

During the Ordovician period, between 500 and 440 million years ago, the majority of the continents were joined together in a gigantic supercontinent called Gondwana, located near the equator. In the seas, trilobites, of which there were many species, continued to dominate. The mollusk population also developed very significantly. ▸▸

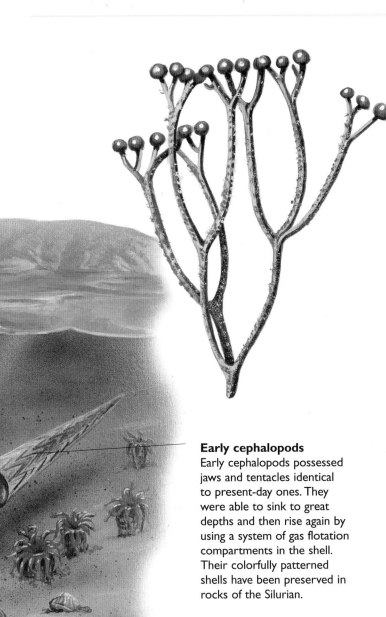

Cooksonia* and *Baragwanathia
Cooksonia (left) and *Baragwanathia* (right) were among the earliest plants to colonize dry land. Dating to the Silurian, they are the earliest known vascular plants, that is to say, plants equipped with tissues for distributing nutrients. These organisms had a complex structure, including a stem and leaves, but no flowers. They reproduced by means of spores.

Early cephalopods
Early cephalopods possessed jaws and tentacles identical to present-day ones. They were able to sink to great depths and then rise again by using a system of gas flotation compartments in the shell. Their colorfully patterned shells have been preserved in rocks of the Silurian.

THE FRONTIERS OF KNOWLEDGE

WHERE DID VERTEBRATES EVOLVE?

Experts have not yet definitively ascertained whether vertebrates evolved in a marine or a freshwater environment. The earliest fish fossils come from ocean sediments, but most of the evidence dating from the Silurian onward has been found in freshwater environments.

Fossils: how they form, how they are dated

Fossils are the remains of animal and plant organisms that lived on Earth in the past, which have been preserved to the present day. They are of extraordinary importance in puzzling together the history of life on Earth. From the impressions, footprints, and fossilized skeletons left by extinct animals, it is possible to ascertain their behavior and structure as well as to reconstruct the environments in which they lived.

STORIES AND PIONEERS OF SCIENCE

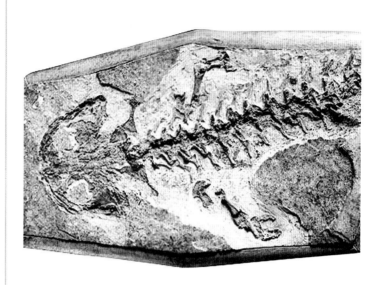

HOMO DILUVII TESTIS

Scientists in the eighteenth century did not believe that fossils were animals or plants that had lived in the past; rather they attributed the remains to victims of the biblical Flood. The Swiss scholar Johann Scheuchzer was also convinced of this, and in 1731 he announced the discovery of a fossil which, in his view, left no room for doubt.
He called it Homo diluvii testis *("man who witnessed the Flood"). In actual fact it was an enormous salamander that lived 8 million years ago.*

Death of an organism
The formation of a fossil from the remains of a living being is a rare process; it may begin, for example, when a dead organism sinks onto the seabed.

Burial
Normally animal or plant remains decompose completely in the space of a few years. For this not to happen, they must be quickly covered by muddy sediment, which prevents the destructive action of decomposing agents.

Consumption and mineralization
The soft parts of the body are destroyed very slowly. The hard parts, on the other hand, become impregnated with minerals thanks to a more or less complete molecule exchange with the water circulating in the sediment. Replacement of the hard elements of the organism by minerals takes a long time and sometimes occurs molecule by molecule. This preserves the internal structure of the organism as well.

Uncovering
Because of movements of the Earth's crust, the remains of organisms trapped in sedimentary rocks (the only kind that can preserve fossils) may reappear on the surface.

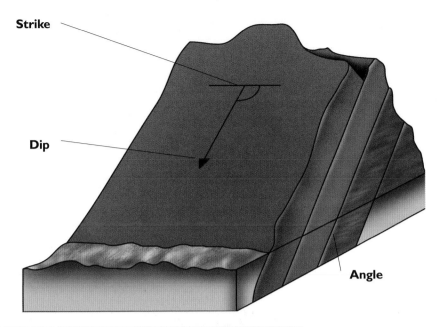

Strike

Dip

Angle

Rock attitude

Extensive areas of the Earth's surface that contain fossils today are made up of layers of rock deposited in the sea over past eras. Establishing the exact arrangement of the layers, that is to say the attitude, is a necessary step in calculating the age of the fossils found in the rock.

To work out the exact attitude, geologists consider three aspects of a layer:

1. Strike—the line of intersection of the layer with a horizontal plane.
2. Dip—the direction perpendicular to the strike.
3. Angle—the inclination of the layer relative to the horizontal plane.

THE AGE DATING OF ROCKS

A rock's age can be established by attributing it to a geological period characterized by a particular event like glaciation or a drop in the sea level. This system is based on the study of fossils. Instead, another method examines the radioactive isotopes (atoms with the same number of protons but a different number of neutrons) of certain elements contained in rocks. Isotopes are transformed into other elements over a set period of time. For example, uranium isotopes become lead; those of a particular type of carbon turn into nitrogen.

By studying how these changes take place, and the extent to which they occur, it is possible to establish the age of the rock.

The history of the Earth

Some mollusks, so-called nautiloids (cephalopods with a spiral-shaped shell), were sometimes several yards long. Ostracoderms, the primitive ancestors of fish, also developed, and there was the first appearance of creatures like echinoderms and graptolites, tiny marine organisms. Toward the end of the Ordovician, part of Gondwana, formed by what is today Africa, South America, Australia, India, and the Antarctic, moved toward the South Pole and was covered by glaciers. This was the so-called Ordovician ice age.

The move to dry land

When the cold temperatures of the Ordovician ice age had passed, there occurred another incredibly important phenomenon in the history of living beings. The waters of lakes and seas receded, which in all likelihood left a number of plants high and dry. Some plants, partially exposed to the air, managed to survive and began to populate the shores.

During the Silurian, the period between 440 and 395 million years ago, life was finally appearing on land. This was made possible above all by the photosynthesizing organisms of the oceans, which over the course of millions of years had enriched the atmosphere with oxygen and made it breathable. ▶▶

The fish age

In the same period in which plants and invertebrates first made their appearance on dry land, a revolution also took place in the seas. A new group of animals evolved that gradually differentiated into numerous species: fish.

Climatius
This small acanthodian fish was less than 4 inches (10 cm) long. Its many pairs of fins made it a good swimmer, and several spines on its stomach protected it from predators.

Dunkleosteus
This gigantic placoderm was more than 10 feet (3 m) long. It had a massive bite and was a fair match for a shark.

Gemuendina
This placoderm resembled present-day skates, which are, however, cartilaginous fish that evolved millions of years later.

The history of the Earth

The presence of oxygen was exploited by the first "conquerors" of dry land, which were protected from solar ultraviolet radiation by formation of the ozone layer. The same problems faced by plants, including reproduction and dehydration, were overcome not too long afterward by the first animals to follow plants onto dry land. These were herbivorous invertebrates, and initially they enjoyed a predator-free environment. But the good times did not last long because carnivorous terrestrial arthropods, similar to present-day spiders and scorpions, soon arrived as well.
From a geological point of view, there were movements between the European and North American landmasses toward the end of the Silurian; these gave rise to an impressive mountain chain; the Scandinavian mountains and the Scottish Highlands are remains of this chain. The zones that would later form into the Urals also began to be thrust upward.
While life was finally becoming established on land, in the oceans the vertebrates originating in the Ordovician and Silurian developed forms with new characteristics.

A revolutionary jaw

About 440 million years ago, aquatic animals called acanthodians (also ancestors of fish) first appeared. They were the first animals equipped with a jaw, a kind of pincer enabling the mouth to grab and crush its prey. ▶▶

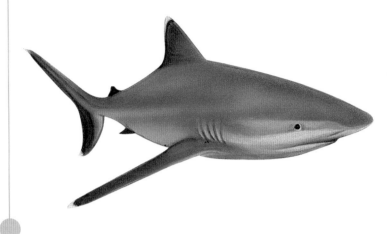

A GIANT IN PERIL

Sharks have a reputation for being man-eaters. In actual fact, the majority of species are harmless to humans, and they are all important from an ecological point of view, given the role they play at the top of the food pyramid. Unfortunately, many of them are at risk of extinction. The great white shark, the most notorious and feared of all shark species, is now protected in Australia, Tasmania, South Africa, and California and along the Atlantic coast. But that is not enough to save it. Many biologists have called for a world treaty to ban indiscriminate killing and to preserve their habitat.

Sharks

Sharks are very ancient animals. The earliest fossils date back 390 million years. Although evolution has experimented with them in various forms since then, the basic model has proved to be a winner and is extremely versatile. They still exist today and are not that different from their Devonian ancestors.

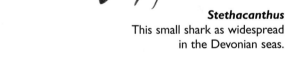

Stethacanthus
This small shark as widespread in the Devonian seas.

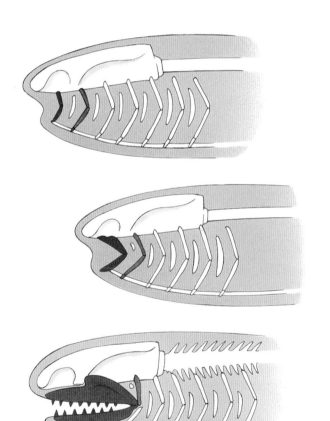

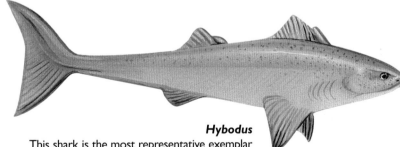

Hybodus
This shark is the most representative exemplar of the second period in which sharks spread widely, which took place in the Mesozoic.

The development of jaws
Jaws may have originated from bony plates protecting the heads of the earliest acanthodians. Through chance mutation and natural selection, they gradually became an instrument for trapping, crushing, and chewing prey.

Cladoselache
This shark was a frightening predator in the Devonian.

The first vascular plants

The first mosses had already appeared on the Earth's surface 440 million years ago. A layer of insulation protected them from dehydration, and they reproduced by releasing ovules and spermatozoids in rainwater. They did not rise more than an inch or two from the ground because they had no stems. The first modern-looking plants, that is, with roots, stems, and leaves, appeared almost 100 million years later.

Vascular plants
Vascular plants have evolved in widely different forms, both in shape and in the pattern of their roots and leaves. However, they all share a common structure: a stem that supports the plant and distributes water and useful substances through the whole body.

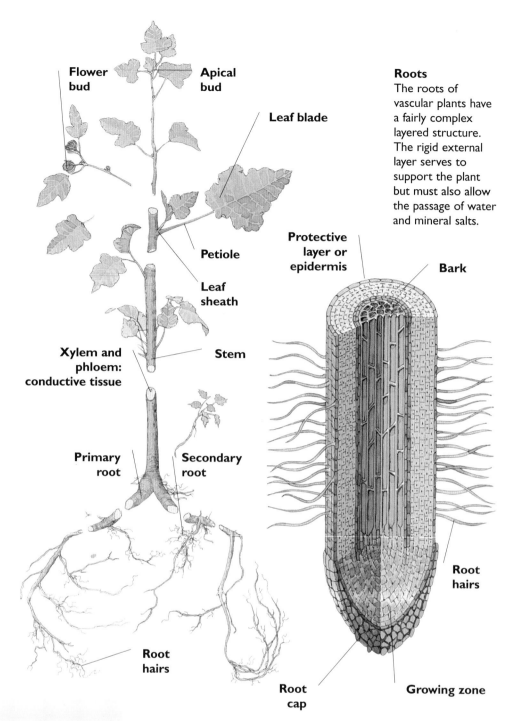

Flower bud

Apical bud

Leaf blade

Roots
The roots of vascular plants have a fairly complex layered structure. The rigid external layer serves to support the plant but must also allow the passage of water and mineral salts.

Petiole

Leaf sheath

Protective layer or epidermis

Bark

Xylem and phloem: conductive tissue

Stem

Primary root

Secondary root

Root hairs

Root hairs

Root cap

Growing zone

The history of the Earth

Descendants of acanthodians developed jaws with teeth, which were even more fearsome hunting instruments. Animals with these hard, sharp teeth emerged about 395 million years ago during the Devonian period, which lasted about 50 million years. Apart from the acanthodians, armor-plated fish called placoderms also spread; in some cases these reached up to 30 feet in length.
Besides the birth of the predecessors of present-day fish, the Devonian also saw the spread of ammonites, marine invertebrates that were to play a key role in life on Earth for about 300 million years.
Meanwhile, numerous changes were underway on dry land.

Earthquakes and volcanic eruptions, together with periods of violent rainfall and drought, caused the formation of vast pools in which plant life, especially ferns, flourished.
In many continental zones the climate was hot. Amphibians also appeared, the first step toward the development of vertebrates on land.

Amphibians and forests

Amphibians faced many difficulties in establishing themselves on land. But once these had been overcome, they dominated Earth until the end of the Paleozoic, when they were superseded by reptiles. ▸▸

THE PETRIFICATION OF FORESTS

The structure of vascular plants is such that they fossilize easily. Some very ancient forests can still be seen today in the shape of petrified trees, as at Dunarobba in central Italy. In the past this phenomenon was an enigma for scholars. Recent research has begun to unravel the mystery:

In woods that become buried in layers of sediment, certain silicon-based compounds sometimes replace the organic substances contained in the cells of leaves and stems, while leaving the microscopic structure and the appearance of the plants intact.

From early vascular plants to bushes and trees

Psilophytes and rhyniophytes were the most primitive vascular plants. Gymnosperms and angiosperms, as shown in the tree of evolution, were more advanced.

Archaeopteris

According to many experts, this was the first large tree in history and formed the first forests. It appeared on Earth 380 million years ago.

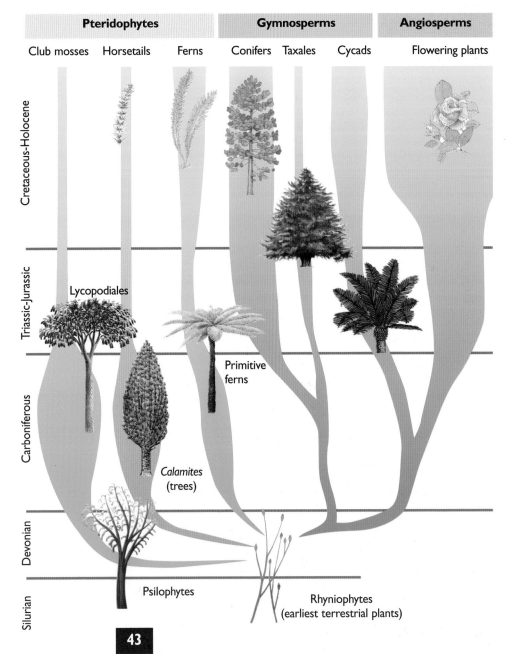

Pteridophytes			Gymnosperms			Angiosperms
Club mosses	Horsetails	Ferns	Conifers	Taxales	Cycads	Flowering plants

Cretaceous-Holocene

Triassic-Jurassic

Lycopodiales

Primitive ferns

Carboniferous

Calamites (trees)

Devonian

Psilophytes

Rhyniophytes (earliest terrestrial plants)

Silurian

The first terrestrial vertebrates

In the Devonian, earthquakes and volcanic eruptions had caused some areas to emerge from the sea and others to sink into it. Pond and marsh areas were formed. The fish living there had to find a way of adapting to dry periods, to learn to spend a little time out of the water or to move from one pool to another. This was achieved, during the Carboniferous, through the elimination of gills, the development of new ways of absorbing the oxygen required for breathing, and the transformation of fins into organs for locomotion on land. Amphibians had arrived.

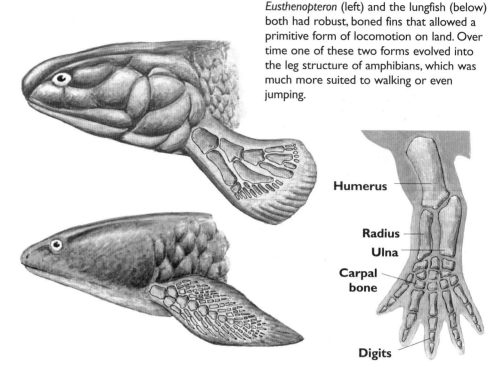

From fins to legs
Eusthenopteron (left) and the lungfish (below) both had robust, boned fins that allowed a primitive form of locomotion on land. Over time one of these two forms evolved into the leg structure of amphibians, which was much more suited to walking or even jumping.

Humerus
Radius
Ulna
Carpal bone
Digits

Ichtyostega
This organism was one the first that can really be defined as an amphibian. Although it still had a fish tail, the skeleton structure enabled it to live on land. It was not covered in scales but had a smooth, constantly damp skin.

Eusthenopteron
This fish breathed in air above the water's surface by swallowing it. The esophagus contained lots of blood vessels, which absorbed and circulated oxygen. The fins, positioned under the body, enabled it to drag itself along on dry land for short distances.

Lungfish
In the first fish of this type, the skull consisted of a solid bone casing. The present-day relative of the same family reveals the stratagem that may also have been used by the early progenitors of amphibians: It is capable of alternating branchial respiration and a rudimentary form of lung respiration.

Reptiles appeared about 330 million years ago, during the Carboniferous. This period ran from 345 to 280 million years ago and took its name from the vast fossil carbon deposits that originated during that time and which are still exploited by humans today.

Toward the end of the Carboniferous, the Appalachian mountain chain formed, stretching along the eastern coast of North America from Canada to the southern United States. The formation of these mountains was part of a massive process. In fact, the continent of Gondwana was moving northward, where it collided with another large landmass called Laurasia (Asia and Europe combined). Then all the areas of existing dry land began to join together into a single supercontinent called Pangaea.

The Permian

The formation of Pangaea was completed in the Permian, the period that ended the Paleozoic era. A gigantic mass of land extended from one pole to the other. Along the equator, between Laurasia and the northern part of Gondwana, was a large expanse of water called the Tethys Sea.

The climate was not the same everywhere. The southern hemisphere was in the grip of an ice age that had begun at the end of the Carboniferous. Ice had covered the Antarctic, India, southern Australia, and a large part of Africa and South America. In the central section of the planet there was a prevalently hot, humid climate.

Mudskipper
This small fish is common in mangrove forests. Like early amphibians, it can push itself out of the water on its fins and breathe through its skin.

THE FRONTIERS OF KNOWLEDGE

WHY ARE FROGS DISAPPEARING?

For years now no one has been able to find a Costa Rican golden toad. It seems to have become extinct, and with it many species of frogs and toads from Australia to the Amazon, from the United States to Asia. The causes of the dramatic decline in the number of these amphibians are still quite mysterious; scientists around the world are trying to solve the mystery, which could give us much valuable information about the health of our planet.

The Carboniferous forests

The Carboniferous, the period that ran from 345 to 280 million years ago, witnessed an incredible development in plant life, which was favored by a hot, humid climate. Vast, luxuriant forests of giant treelike club mosses thrived on the edge of marshes. The ground was covered by smaller plants and ferns populated by crawling millipedes the size of snakes. The proliferation of flora was accompanied by that of fauna. Many giant insects buzzed around in the air, numerous forms of arthropods and fish became widespread, and the first amphibians appeared.

Stenodictya
The most interesting aspect of this primitive insect, no more than 4 inches (10 cm) long, was a third pair of small wings on the sides of the head, which functioned as sensory organs.

Flora in the Carboniferous
Giant club mosses, horsetails, and arboreal ferns like *Rhacophyton* populated the forests, which mainly grew along the edge of marsh areas.

Arthropleura armata
This arthropod was very similar to a millipede, but about 6 feet (1.8 m) long.

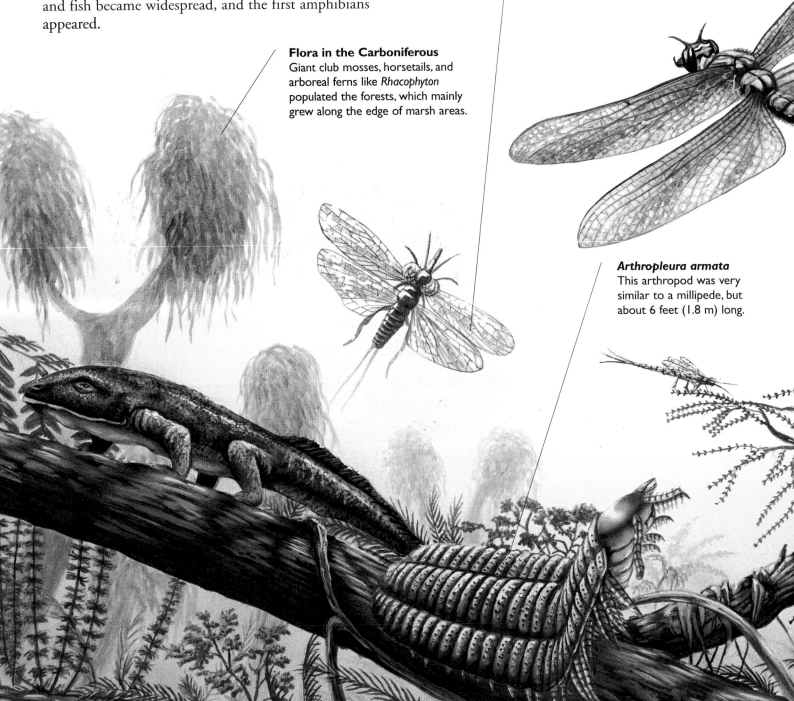

On both sides of the equator there were endless stretches of desert where only scorpions and a few other creatures could survive. In the northern part of Pangaea, it was cold and dry.

New species of insects, including beetles, established themselves in the forests during the Permian. The oceans continued to be dominated by fish, and amphibians and early reptiles gradually spread through swamp regions. Everything seemed to favor the thriving of living forms, but then something apocalyptic took place, something that has still not been fully explained but that resulted in a mass extinction. It was not the first time this occurred nor would it be

the last, but it was probably the most devastating period of extinction in the history of our planet.

The catastrophe of the Permian

According to some experts, in just 1 million years (a mere instant in geological time), more than 80% of all the species living on Earth became extinct. Vertebrates and invertebrates, plants and aquatic and terrestrial animals were all affected. It is estimated that 90% of all the species living in the oceans during the Permian did not survive into the Mesozoic. About 78% of reptile and 67% of amphibian families were lost.

Meganeura
Very similar to present-day dragonflies but of gigantic dimensions. Its wingspan was about 27 inches (70 cm).

THE FRONTIERS OF KNOWLEDGE

SCIENCE-FICTION ARTHROPODS

The extraordinary development of arthropods during the Carboniferous led to the appearance of enormous species that seemed to defy biological and physical laws. Scientists are still amazed by the extraordinary characteristics of these animals. For example, the protective coating of some beetles consists of one of the most resistant *substances known, which has even been studied for possible military applications. Some Japanese and American scientists are even trying to create "cyborg" arthropods worthy of a science-fiction world. A microchip is installed in the nervous system to make them semirobotic and remote-controlled.*

The origin of oil and coal

The oil and coal we use for energy were formed in the course of events that began hundreds of millions of years ago. Oil originated from the sedimentation of microorganisms that populated the seas of the Ordovician about 450 million years ago. Coal, on the other hand, derives from the enormous mass of plant life that flourished in the forests of the Carboniferous. When plants died, they were decomposed by bacteria and slowly transformed into various qualities of coal.

The hunt for black gold
To determine where there is the greatest likelihood of finding oil fields, experts rely on special techniques for X-raying underground as well as on studies of a given area's geological characteristics. For example, geologists can measure the magnetic properties of rocks for variations resulting from the presence of such a field. Definitive proof of the existence of an oil field can be obtained only by drilling deep underground.

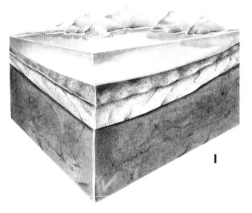
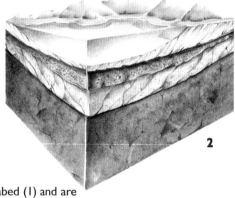
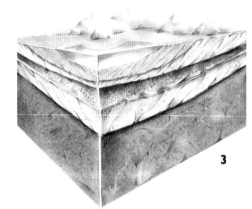

From sediments to oil
The remains of organisms accumulate on the seabed (1) and are subsequently covered by sand and other sediments (2). In order to be transformed into oil, the remains of these microorganisms need to be subjected to high pressures and temperatures (3). These conditions are achieved when, over the course of millions of years, new detritus pushes the remains down even further, to depths of sometimes a mile or more.

The history of the Earth

Trilobites, which had diversified over the course of 250 million years into at least 15,000 species, would never again swim in the oceans. Recently it has been suggested that life was almost completely swept away by the collision of a meteorite with the Earth. The impact made by an asteroid 5 or 6 miles in diameter would have caused an environmental cataclysm. This theory, however, is still being debated. According to many scientists the real cause of the catastrophe was a sudden increase in volcanic activity, with millions of tons of lava pouring out onto the Earth's surface. In this scenario, smoke would have filled the atmosphere with gases and dust, darkening the sky and provoking major climatic changes.

Other geologists and paleontologists argue that there was no single cause. In their view, a determinant role was played not only by climatic change but also by variations in sea levels and by continental drift. These are recurrent arguments that are also used to explain other mass extinctions.
The fact remains that about 200 million years ago the Earth once again became a pretty desolate place. Yet despite everything, the embers of life were still burning. The survivors would soon take advantage of having been spared and would repopulate the land and the sea. In fact, the Permian catastrophe opened the way to the undisputed dominators of the Mesozoic: dinosaurs.

ALTERNATIVE ENERGY SOURCES

Alternative energy sources, like those deriving from the Sun, the heat of the Earth, or even from garbage, are being used to only a limited extent. With time, however, they could become increasingly important if the cost of fossil fuels, in both economic and environmental terms, becomes unsustainable. One of the areas of greatest research and development concerns the use of wind turbines, which exploit wind power and have an extremely limited impact on the environment.

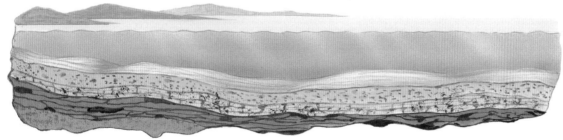

Peat
Large forests of dense, luxuriant trees grow alongside or in swamps and marshes, or in other environments where oxygen-starved water prevents bacteria from decomposing them when they fall and accumulate underwater. Plant remains can clearly be recognized in the resulting peat.

Lignite
The peat is covered by clay and sand transported by water. New trees and leaves are deposited on top, and the weight of the material pushes the plant layers downward, where they are transformed over time into lignite, a soft, low-grade coal.

Anthracite
If lignite is pushed even deeper, the pressure and temperature become so great that it is gradually transformed into anthracite, the most highly prized form of coal, which is 90% carbon.

Chapter 3
The age of the dinosaurs

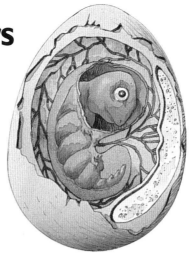

The amniotic egg
The amniotic egg contains four membranes (the amnion, the yolk sac, the allantois, and the chorion), which protect the embryo from bumps and dehydration and allow the flow of nourishment, metabolic waste, and gases. Eggs laid by reptiles have a rigid, porous shell that protects the embryo from dehydration but permits respiration.

One of the greatest catastrophes of all time befell the Earth 245 million years ago. Yet the seas and lands were not unpopulated, and thanks to chance mutations and the pressure of natural selection, the survivors were ready to colonize the world with a new and explosive proliferation of life forms. This was the beginning of the Mesozoic era, which was to last 180 million years and would see the appearance of two totally new classes of animals: mammals and birds. But the real dominators of the planet, on land, in the air, and in the water, would be the reptiles. They had already made an appearance in the Carboniferous period, having successfully overcome the extraordinary challenge of how to survive outside water.

Scales
The skin of reptiles has no glands and is covered with scales to provide protection from dehydration while allowing flexibility and agility of movement. Saurians and snakes have to shed their outer layer of skin as they grow, whereas tortoises and crocodiles have large scales that grow in concentric rings; the number of rings is approximately proportionate to age.

Locomotion
Life on land also required the evolution of a more robust skeletal structure that could support the body's weight out of water and make movement easier. Many orders of reptiles developed limbs positioned vertically below, rather than to the sides of, the body, becoming the first vertebrates capable of lifting their bellies off the ground.

The lung

Amphibians had already developed lungs, enabling them to breathe out of water (gills would have dried out). The lung provides a way of keeping a space inside the body wet with a constant flow of blood; through it, oxygen and carbon dioxide can be exchanged with the atmosphere. The lung was perfected by reptiles. Respiration, by means of the expansion and compression of a thoracic cage, also improved.

Mating out of water

Unlike in fish and amphibians, fertilization (the union between the male sperm and the female egg) in reptiles takes place internally through penetration. For this reason, it can also occur on land.

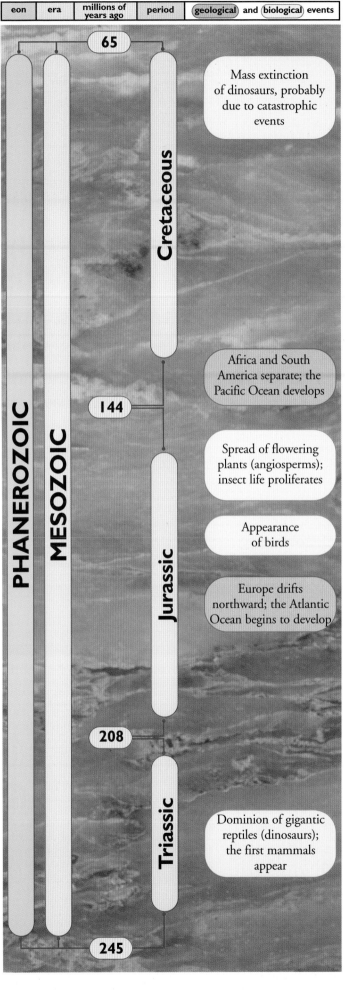

eon	era	millions of years ago	period	geological and biological events
		65		
			Cretaceous	Mass extinction of dinosaurs, probably due to catastrophic events
				Africa and South America separate; the Pacific Ocean develops
		144		
			Jurassic	Spread of flowering plants (angiosperms); insect life proliferates
				Appearance of birds
				Europe drifts northward; the Atlantic Ocean begins to develop
		208		
PHANEROZOIC	MESOZOIC		Triassic	Dominion of gigantic reptiles (dinosaurs); the first mammals appear
		245		

Reptiles

Not many people like reptiles, and many are afraid or disgusted when they come across a lizard or snake. Yet we are all descended from reptiles, and they still fulfill a fundamental role in many ecosystems today. There are currently about 6,000 known species, most of which live in hot or temperate regions.

Not just dinosaurs
When we think of the large reptiles of the past, we imagine dinosaurs. But there were many other groups. Pelycosaurs, for instance, like these *Dimetrodon*, had large sail-like crests on their backs. According to some scientists, they acted as radiators to regulate body temperature—when the animals needed to warm themselves, they exposed them to the Sun, and when it was too hot, they could be used in the shade to release excess heat. However, some paleontologists argue that the crests were used in mating rituals by adult males.

THE FRONTIERS OF KNOWLEDGE

SMELLING ... WITH THE TONGUE

Reptiles, especially snakes, do not sense odors just through their noses. Their darting tongues gather odorous particles from the air and ground and bring them in contact with a special scent organ known as Jacobson's organ or vomeronasal cartilage. Scientists have discovered that humans have this organ as well, inside the nose. Some experts argue that it is not used to sense ordinary odors but pheromones, which are similar to sexual hormones; these substances are capable of altering the rhythm of our heartbeat as well as our emotional state.

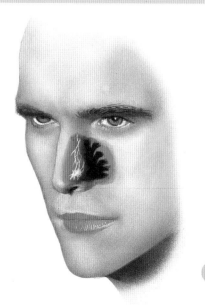

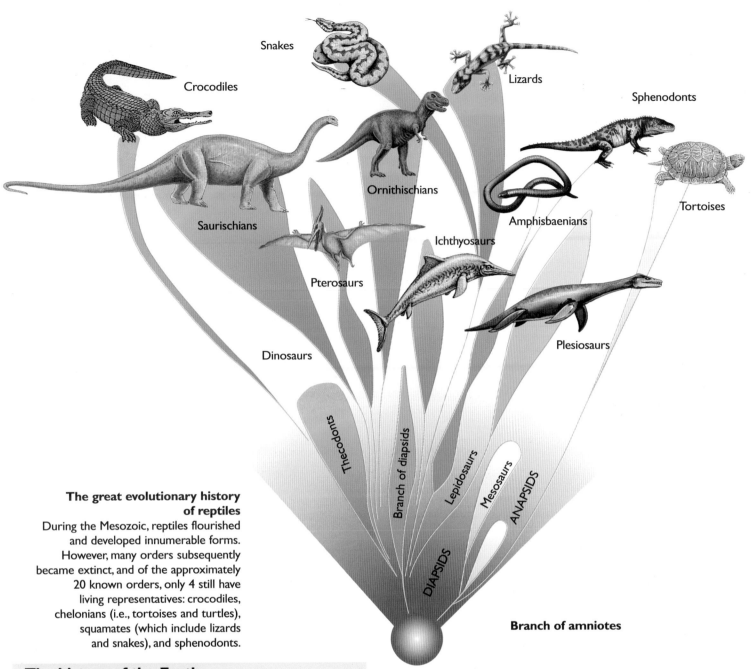

Snakes

Crocodiles

Lizards

Sphenodonts

Ornithischians

Saurischians

Amphisbaenians

Tortoises

Ichthyosaurs

Pterosaurs

Dinosaurs

Plesiosaurs

Thecodonts

Branch of diapsids

Lepidosaurs

Mesosaurs

ANAPSIDS

The great evolutionary history of reptiles
During the Mesozoic, reptiles flourished and developed innumerable forms. However, many orders subsequently became extinct, and of the approximately 20 known orders, only 4 still have living representatives: crocodiles, chelonians (i.e., tortoises and turtles), squamates (which include lizards and snakes), and sphenodonts.

DIAPSIDS

Branch of amniotes

The history of the Earth

After the disaster … life

In order to understand why, in the wake of a mass extinction, the surviving organisms manage to differentiate over just a few dozen million years and produce an extraordinary variety of forms, it is important to know a little about the concept of an ecological niche. The habitat of a living being is its "address" within an ecosystem (on a blade of grass, on a shallow seabed, in forest undergrowth, and so on). The ecological niche, on the other hand, involves the "job" an organism carries out in its environment. For example, the habitat of an oak may be Mediterranean vegetation or forest, but its ecological niche is the sum of the functions it performs in relation to other inhabitants of the habitat, for instance: absorbing light, carbon dioxide, and water; emitting oxygen; producing cellulose and sugars; absorbing water and mineral salts; and interacting with other organisms in various mutually beneficial ways. When a species in a given ecosystem becomes extinct, it clearly stops performing a series of necessary functions and using certain exploitable resources. Competition between the surviving organisms, combined with the mechanism of chance mutation, is such that creatures that happen to be capable of profiting in some way from the vacant niche will be at an advantage. With time these organisms differentiate and evolve into new species capable of performing some or all of the roles previously carried out by the extinct species. ▶▶

Therapsids

Therapsids, or "mammalian reptiles," lived on Earth for 70 million years. From the structure of the jaw and skull and the differentiation of the teeth (incisors, canines), we can glean that they were the progenitors of mammals. Some of them probably had fur, and they were among the first warm-blooded animals; in other words, they were able to maintain a constant body temperature.

Ferocious predators
Some therapsids, like *Lycaenops* and *Cynognathus*, were carnivores. We can deduce this from their long canines and sharp incisive teeth, ideal for killing prey and tearing off strips of flesh.

The history of the Earth

Occupation of a vacant ecological niche by new species is called colonization. This took place in the Mesozoic; the disappearance of a huge number of organisms left many ecological niches vacant, and new species appeared to occupy them.

At the beginning of the Mesozoic, the climate of the immense Pangaea continent was generally hot, sea levels were high, and the majority of dry land, especially inland, was desert. In areas with plant life, there were no grassy fields, flowers, or fruit trees because these had not yet evolved. The main trees were conifers like sequoias, araucarias, and pines.

The seas were populated by ammonites, urchins, various kinds of mollusks, archaic sharks, and certain bony fish.

On land, insects became increasingly widespread, and the first flies appeared. Among the vertebrates, there were lots of amphibians. Some, like certain labyrinthodonts, were up to 16 feet (5 m) in length. However, the animals that diversified most extraordinarily were reptiles.

From reptiles to mammals

Driven by the mechanism of casual mutation and by natural selection, reptiles gradually occupied most of the ecological niches left vacant after the Permian mass extinction. One group in particular, therapsids, had been decimated, yet the surviving species prospered for much of the Mesozoic. ▸▸

Placid herbivores

Many therapsids were herbivorous and developed a powerful jaw to shred the leathery horsetail plants. *Moschops*, which died out before the Permian catastrophe, had feet with five webbed digits and probably lived in swampy areas. *Lystrosaurus*, on the other hand, just had two long tusks. It lived in oases and swamps rich in vegetation and led a life similar to that of present-day hippopotami.

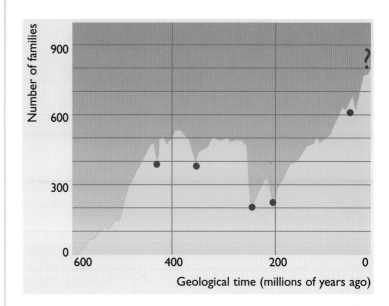

Number of families — Geological time (millions of years ago)

FIVE MAJOR MASS EXTINCTIONS. PLUS ONE?

Life has never been peaceful on Earth. It has been marked by at least a dozen mass extinctions, and each time the surviving organisms diversified to colonize the vacant ecological niches. There have been five major extinctions in the planet's history, but some biologists claim we are currently witnessing the sixth.

This, they say, is being directly caused by human activity, which is transforming the Earth's ecosystems so radically and quickly that living creatures cannot adapt. There is heated debate about this issue, and the data are inconclusive. What will be the real extent of the sixth extinction?

290 million years ago

245 million years ago

The Permian: a catastrophe, but not for all everyone

Not all therapsids perished in the Permian mass extinction. Some, like *Moschops*, had already become extinct. Others continued to proliferate during the Triassic, giving rise to new species. The retreat of the seas following the Permian catastrophe, which killed off many marine and coastal fauna and caused desertification of immense areas of land, was less devastating for reptiles than for many other vertebrates.

Dinosaurs

Dinosaurs are perhaps the most famous of all reptiles, the "celebrities" of the prehistoric period. Hundreds of genera have been identified, and there were certainly many more. Some paleontologists talk in terms of thousands of species, others of almost half a million, of which very few have left fossil remains.

Dinosaurs for all tastes

At the beginning of the Mesozoic the main primary producers were ferns, conifers, and cycads, whereas the primary consumers among dinosaurs, included *Triceratops*, *Diplodocus*, and *Iguanodon*. The agile *Procompsognathus* and the fearsome *Deinonychus* were secondary consumers. Finally, at the top of the food pyramid, were the tertiary consumers, large carnivores that often preyed on other carnivores. One celebrated example was *Giganotosaurus*.

The food pyramid

Given that any given organism is capable of exploiting between 5% and 20% of the energy potentially available in the food it eats, the primary (plant) producers in any ecosystem must have a much greater mass than that of herbivorous animals (primary consumers), which in turn must be much greater in number than carnivores (secondary consumers), and so forth.

The history of the Earth

Therapsids, also known as "mammalian" reptiles or "paramammals" because in many respects (teeth, skull structure) they were similar to mammals, developed a better sense of hearing, increasingly effective teeth, and a larger brain. Generally they were the size of a large rat or a dog, but some species were as long as 13 feet (4 m). They had probably developed a warm-blooded homeotherm metabolism, that is, the capacity to regulate body temperature fairly independently of the surrounding environment.

Some therapsids, belonging to the suborder of cynodonts, were the progenitors of the earliest true mammals. However, available fossil remains are not sufficient to ascertain how similar the biology of these transitional animals was to that of the mammals we know today. It is not known with certainty if and how they gave birth (instead of laying eggs), whether some of them had mammary glands, and so on. For example, between the end of the Triassic and the beginning of the Jurassic, about 230 million years ago, a cynodont therapsid called *Probainognathus* appeared on the scene. Its skull and jaw were very similar to those of present-day mammals; according to many paleontologists, it was warm-blooded and covered in fur, even though fossil remains do not provide definitive proof. Some warm-blooded therapsids may also have developed sudoriparous glands, similar to those of mammals, which helped to regulate body temperature. ▸▸

Gallimimus

Tyrannosaurus rex

Diplodocus

TYRANNOSAURUS REX, **FEROCIOUS PREDATOR OR SIMPLE GARBAGE COLLECTOR?**

Tyrannosaurus rex *is imagined to be one of the most ferocious predators ever to have inhabited Earth. Yet some people maintain that, in actual fact, it fed only on corpses. Observing the animal's bone structure, size, and weight, some paleontologists have deduced that the tyrannosaur was too slow to be a hunter. Others say it was sufficiently agile to make small jumps and run short distances. It probably did hunt, but only by lying in ambush in the thick forest vegetation.*

Saurischians and ornithischians

Dinosaurs are divided into two large orders, saurischians ("reptile-hipped") and ornithischians ("bird-hipped"). The pubis and ischium (the lower bone of the pelvis) of saurischians were separate and pointed in opposite directions. This order included bipedal carnivores (theropods) and quadrupedal herbivores (giant sauropods). On the other hand, the pubis and ischium of ornithischians were close to each other, parallel, and pointed backward. They were herbivores and included stegosaurs, ankylosaurs, and ceratopsians.

Triceratops

Iguanodon

Dinosaurs with feathers

According to many paleontologists, feathers appeared long before birds did and were not used for flying but for maintaining body heat. Many dinosaur fossils bear traces resembling feathers, and the remains of Dromeosaurus recently uncovered in China show clear signs of a layer of feathers.

Dyoplosaurus

Hypsilophodon

Parental care among dinosaurs

It was not unknown for dinosaurs to look after and bring up their young, and some of them had quite highly developed "family" behavior. Some kinds of newly hatched dinosaurs were probably unable to defend themselves and find food on their own; so their parents cared for them by feeding them berries and shoots until they became independent. The extent of parental care among dinosaurs varied widely, however. It seems, for example, that carnivores taught their young from a very early age the best ways to hunt prey.

Guarding eggs
Dinosaurs guarded their eggs and were probably forced to cover them with their bodies. This hypothesis is supported by the discovery of numerous fossil nests separated from each other by a distance equal to that of an adult animal. Fossils also show that when the mother left the nest, she covered it with leaves and branches to keep the eggs warm and to protect them against predators.

The history of the Earth

Evolution of some sudoriparous glands, which might at first have been licked by the young in order to absorb mineral salts, may have led to development of the first mammary glands.
However, therapsids did not dominate the Earth during the Mesozoic. Nor did mammals, which evolved from them but remained in the background for more than 140 million years; indeed, they risked being swept away by the appearance of new and extraordinary animal families. In the same period in which mammals were evolving from therapsids, another group of reptiles, thecodonts, were giving rise to the creatures that have captured our imagination more than any others—dinosaurs.

The arrival of the "terrible lizards"

Thecodonts had already appeared during the Permian. They were similar in shape to present-day crocodiles but had bony plates beneath their skin. Having survived the catastrophe, they colonized many of the vacant ecological niches. Some returned to aquatic environments and evolved into crocodiles. Others adapted to grazing on land plants, leading to the development of rhynchocephalians, of which there is still one existing species, the tuatara, which lives in New Zealand. Dinosaurs evolved from other thecodonts toward the end of the Triassic. *Deinos sauros* means "terrible lizard" in Greek, though the early dinosaurs probably did not look so very terrible. ▸▸

STUDYING ANIMAL BEHAVIOR THROUGH FOSSILS

The behavior of dinosaurs and other animals that lived in the past can be deduced from fossils. Examining prints left on the ground, skeleton bones, and other paleontological data, experts try to reconstruct the anatomy, biology, and individual and social behavior of these animals.
For example, it is thought that herbivorous dinosaurs lived in groups. This is suggested by the recent discovery of the imprints made by a migrating herd; the young were in the middle, surrounded by a protective circle of adults.

STORIES AND PIONEERS OF SCIENCE

THE MYSTERY OF THE IGUANA TOOTH

In 1822, the paleontologist Mary Ann Woodhouse Mantell discovered the fossil tooth of an herbivore that seemed too old to attribute to a mammal. But when it was shown to the Frenchman Georges Cuvier, the founder of comparative anatomy, he confirmed that it must be a mammal because no other herbivorous reptiles were known.

The issue was settled when Mary Ann's husband, Gideon Mantell, another pioneer in paleontology, learned of the existence of the South American iguana; this herbivorous reptile has teeth similar to those of the fossil discovered by his wife. The extinct reptile was therefore given the name Iguanodon, *that is, "iguana tooth."*

"Affectionate" reptiles
Even today not all reptiles abandon their young. In some species of crocodile, the females remain near the nest until the eggs hatch and, if need be, defend their babies by holding them in their mouths.

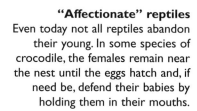

The major dinosaur beds

The fossils of dinosaurs and other large animals were first discovered in ancient times but were taken to be the remains of monsters; the Chinese thought they were "dragons," and the ancient Greeks believed they were the remains of Titans, Giants, Hydras, or Cyclopes. In 1824, William Buckland realized that they were related to extinct animals and scientifically described the first dinosaur fossil, that of *Megalosaurus*. In 1842, Richard Owen coined the term "dinosaur" to denote the entire group. Since then beds of dinosaur fossils have been found all over the world.

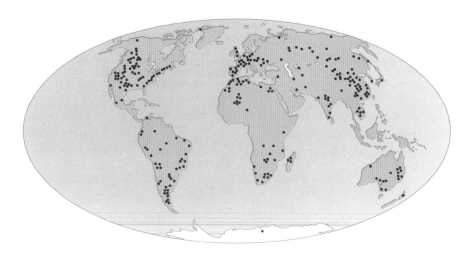

The distribution of finds
There are hundreds of beds of dinosaur fossils. The most spectacular are in the Gobi Desert (Mongolia) and Patagonia (Argentina). Other famous beds are in Canada and in the "dinosaur triangle" straddling Utah and Colorado (United States). Significant dinosaur fossils have been discovered in Europe as well. For instance, hundreds of impressions and entire skeletons have been found in Italy (Friuli-Venezia-Giulia and Apulia).

A paleontological paradise
One of the most spectacular dinosaur beds in the world was recently discovered in Madagascar. Valuable finds included a jaw fragment dating to 230 million years ago, which may have belonged to one of the world's earliest dinosaurs, and the remains of many animals from different classes. These discoveries have helped to reconstruct a Mesozoic ecosystem.

The history of the Earth

One of the first dinosaurs was *Eoraptor*, a small biped not much larger than a turkey and perhaps less intelligent. At the end of the Triassic, 213 million years ago, a minor but not insignificant mass extinction occurred on our planet. A third of all existing animal families were wiped out, including labyrinthodont amphibians, cynodonts, and all marine reptiles except ichthyosaurs. It is not known precisely what triggered this extinction, but it could have been what enabled the dinosaurs and other new reptiles to expand and dominate the Earth.

In the following period, the Jurassic, the continental blocks separated. North America assumed something like its current shape, and South America began to break away from Africa. The climate became drier and more arid; many animals were forced to grow in size and develop extremely long necks in order to reach the foliage on tall plants. Sauropod dinosaurs like *Diplodocus*, *Apatosaurus*, and *Brachiosaurus* were gigantic, slow-moving herbivores as long as 90 feet (27 m) and as tall as a five-story building. They were the most colossal animals ever to have inhabited dry land. Many of these herbivores swallowed gravel and pebbles, known as gastroliths, which they used (through muscular contractions) to chop and grind up plant food in their stomachs. Giant species also developed among carnivorous dinosaurs; allosaurus, for instance, was 39 feet (12 m) long and 16 (5 m) tall. Other species settled at small and intermediate sizes. ▶▶

Fossil hunting
Finding dinosaur fossils is difficult. Paleontologists look for layers of rock dating to the Mesozoic, in areas that at the time were not covered by oceans and were also composed of sedimentary rocks (such as limestone, sandstone, and clay), which permitted the formation of fossils. After finding a fossil, the next step is to free it from the rock. First, picks and shovels are used for digging, followed by an increasingly delicate series of instruments to excavate the final few inches.

A day in Madagascar … in the Cretaceous
Here is a partial reconstruction of an ecosystem during the Cretaceous in Madagascar. A herd of titanosaurs watering on a river bank are attacked by gigantic crocodiles. A carnivorous bird of the *Rahonavis* genus takes advantage of the struggle to feed off the carcasses.

THE FRONTIERS OF KNOWLEDGE

WHERE DID MADAGASCAR COME FROM?

Despite its close vicinity to Africa, Madagascar is a small continent in its own right, both from a geological and a biological point of view. Some experts use dinosaur fossil remains as evidence to support the theory that the island was still connected to India and to the Antarctic during the Cretaceous. According to others, it separated much earlier. Who is right?

Pterosaurs and ichthyosaurs

In the Mesozoic, reptiles colonized the oceans as well. They were not dinosaurs but placodonts, nothosaurs, plesiosaurs, and ichthyosaurs. Some species were 6 feet (1.8 m) long, whereas, others reached as much as 50 feet (15 m). In the meantime, reptiles had also taken to the skies, with the evolution of pterosaurs; they were similar to present-day bats (which are mammals, however) and had membranous wings. Some pterosaurs fed off fish, like pelicans do nowadays, or fruit, like toucans, whereas others were insectivores.

Ramphorhynchus
These animals were the earliest flying reptiles. Some were as small as a sparrow, but others were enormous. The long tail probably served as a rudder and to provide balance during flight.

The history of the Earth

Reptiles also dominated the skies. Pterosaurs appeared, some the size of sparrows, others as imposing as warplanes.

In the meantime, groups of reptiles different from dinosaurs had returned to the marine environments from which their progenitors had emerged. Ichthyosaurs, which lived in the open sea and hunted fish and ammonites, had already appeared by the beginning of the Mesozoic. Then there were placodonts, which fed off bivalve mollusks near the coasts, and nothosaurs, curious-looking animals with long necks and webbed, ducklike feet, which probably lived on sea rocks and hunted fish, a bit like walruses do nowadays.

Major developments: feathers and flowers

Toward the end of the Jurassic, between 150 and 140 million years ago, two extraordinary evolutionary developments took place. A strange dinosaur called *Archaeopteryx*, which was perhaps no longer really a dinosaur, began to glide around among the treetops. It was a flying animal with feathers. At about the same period, somewhat overshadowed by big trees and dinosaurs but of fundamental importance for the history of life, small flowers probably bloomed for the first time. It was a winning development. In the space of a few dozen million years, by the end of the Mesozoic, the majority of living plants were angiosperms, that is, flowering plants. ▸▸

Pterodactyls

Pterodactyls appeared after *Rhamphorhynchus*. They had a short tail and varied greatly in size. The wingspan of *Quetzalcoatlus* (opposite) was at least 36 feet (11 m).

FLYING OR GLIDING

Pterosaur wings consisted of a membrane stretched along the fourth digit, which was enormously long. According to some scientists, the wing could be closed up like an umbrella to enable pterosaurs to use their stumpy limbs to walk on land.

Others think it is more likely that large pterosaurs never came down to land. There has been a lot of discussion about their flying ability: Some paleontologists believe that the largest species could only glide.

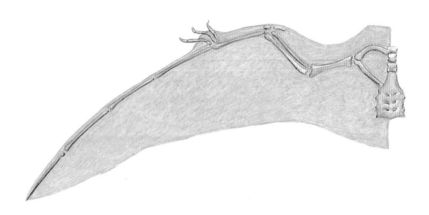

Henodus

Henodus was one of the strangest of all placodonts. Its body, covered by a bony-plated carapace, made it look like a sea turtle.

Ichthyosaurs

Ichthyosaurs were strange reptiles similar to today's dolphins, except that they had both front and back fins. The discovery of fossils containing embryos suggests they did not lay eggs but gave birth to living animals.

Nothosaurs

Ceresiosaurus, fossils of which have been found in Europe, probably swam by moving its body, long neck, and tail in an undulating motion.

Plesiosaurs

Plesiosaur means "ribbon lizard" in Greek. The reason for this name is simple: Some of them had necks that were almost as long as the rest of their bodies.

Dinosaurs on the hunt

Dinosaurs developed various hunting techniques. It is not easy to reconstruct them, but some help comes from fossil remains, especially ones that include both prey and predator, traces of wounds on the bones of large herbivores, and tracks from which one can reconstruct an entire hunting scenario. Some dinosaurs were solitary predators who tracked their prey or lay in ambush. Others organized themselves into groups to kill large herbivores or to surround those that lived in small packs.

What color were they?
Giant dinosaurs had no need either to draw attention to or to camouflage themselves and were probably neutral in color. Smaller dinosaurs would have used camouflage colors, but in the mating season the males might have displayed colored stripes or patches. Poisonous or disgusting animals may have had bright colors to ward off attackers. The coloring of some species may have helped to regulate body temperature: Light colors reflect the heat; dark ones absorb it.

The intelligence of dinosaurs
Some paleontologists have even gone so far as to estimate the IQ of dinosaurs; their deductions are based on the size of the animals' brains in relation to body mass and lifestyle. The most stupid were sauropods, whereas *Velociraptor* and *Deinonychus* were among the most intelligent.

How long did dinosaurs live?
Studying the bones and estimating the growth rate of these large reptiles, some scientists have reached the conclusion that sauropods, like *Diplodocus* and *Apatosaurus*, could have lived for about 200 years. However, there is still debate about this.

The blossoming of the first flowers

There had been plant life on Earth for more than 300 million years, and forests had existed for 200 million years before evolution came up with flowering plants, or angiosperms. These gradually diversified and spread all over the planet toward the middle of the Cretaceous. This was favored by climatic changes that resulted in a greater differentiation between the seasons. The flower was an extraordinary development, but it could function perfectly only with the help of animals. In order to pollinate, flowering plants developed colors, scents, and nectars of all kinds to attract insects (and other animals); these in turn evolved to make use of the nectar.

Sequoia

Cycad

Flora in the Mesozoic
At the beginning of the Mesozoic the landscape was dominated by four groups of flowerless plants: ferns, cycads, cycadeoids (now extinct), and conifers, some of which have remained almost unvaried to the present day. Then angiosperms began to flower, and by the end of the Cretaceous they had become the dominant group.

Fern

THE FRONTIERS OF KNOWLEDGE

PHARMACEUTICALS IN FLOWERS

Not only do the flowers of angiosperms produce nectar and scented substances, but as a defense against predators, many angiosperms have complex, toxic compounds. However, these can be very useful in medicine. The flowers of some members of the poppy family contain opiates (like morphine); those of broom and foxglove (right) have cardiotonic properties; those of the nightshade family (including tobacco, potato, tomato, and eggplant) contain alkaloids, hallucinogens, analgesics, and relaxants.

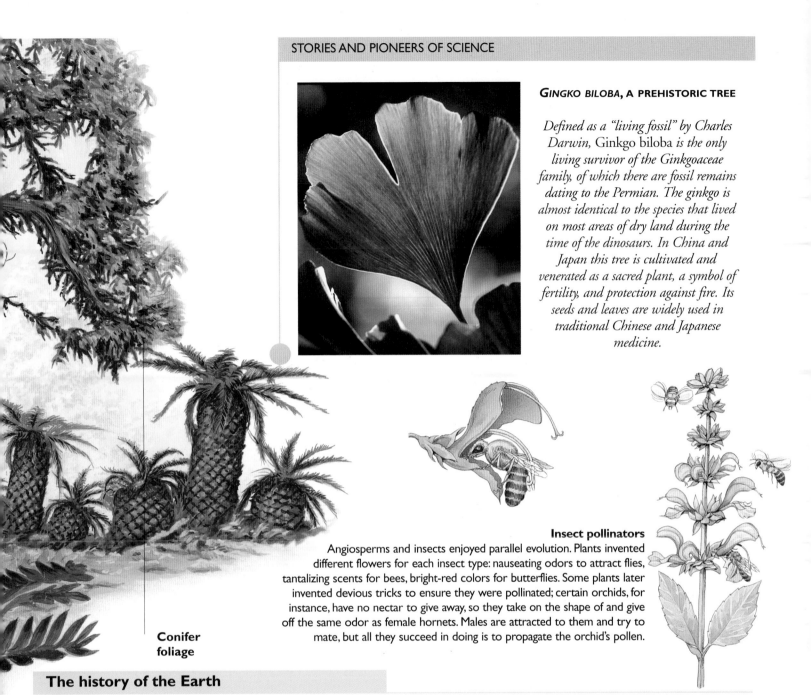

GINGKO BILOBA, A PREHISTORIC TREE

Defined as a "living fossil" by Charles Darwin, Ginkgo biloba *is the only living survivor of the Ginkgoaceae family, of which there are fossil remains dating to the Permian. The ginkgo is almost identical to the species that lived on most areas of dry land during the time of the dinosaurs. In China and Japan this tree is cultivated and venerated as a sacred plant, a symbol of fertility, and protection against fire. Its seeds and leaves are widely used in traditional Chinese and Japanese medicine.*

Insect pollinators
Angiosperms and insects enjoyed parallel evolution. Plants invented different flowers for each insect type: nauseating odors to attract flies, tantalizing scents for bees, bright-red colors for butterflies. Some plants later invented devious tricks to ensure they were pollinated; certain orchids, for instance, have no nectar to give away, so they take on the shape of and give off the same odor as female hornets. Males are attracted to them and try to mate, but all they succeed in doing is to propagate the orchid's pollen.

Conifer foliage

The history of the Earth

Major innovations in the Cretaceous

At the end of the Jurassic, there was another small-scale extinction. Stegosaurs, many sauropods, and numerous species of ammonites and bivalve mollusks were wiped out. But in the Cretaceous, the next geological period, many new organisms appeared, including the "star" dinosaur, *Tyrannosaurus rex*, and *Giganotosaurus* (found a few years ago), which was even bigger and more monstrous. New herbivores included *Triceratops*, which led a lifestyle similar to that of present-day rhinos. The period also witnessed the appearance of the first snakes, which have survived to the present day, as well as the first placental mammals. Birds spread all over the planet:

Toothed birds, now extinct, appeared, as did many species closely resembling cormorants, pelicans, flamingos, and ibis. New flowering plants included magnolias, saxifrages, viburnum, and ficus, but also poplars, willows, laurels, and plane trees. In the same period, the insect kingdom expanded to include the first butterflies, bees, and ants. The climate was hot and subtropical even at the poles, and the Earth was covered by forests. The seas reached the highest level of all time, with only a few large islands remaining above the surface. The continents slowly assumed shapes similar to the ones they have today. But their slide and shuffle on the mantle was often violent: eruptions and earthquakes shook the Earth, leading to the creation of immense mountain chains. ▶▶

The extinction of the dinosaurs

The most accredited current hypothesis to explain the extinction of the dinosaurs is that the Earth was struck by a meteorite, but there is no lack of objections to this theory. Some scientists emphasize the improbability that just one meteorite, however big, produced an ecological catastrophe leading to the extinction not only of dinosaurs but also of nearly two thirds of all living species. The disappearance of dinosaurs might have been caused by a typical set of ecological dynamics that have been used to explain previous extinctions. It is possible, for instance, that the separation of the continents and the consequent change in climate led to the disappearance of many specific ecological niches to which dinosaurs had adapted.

Nuclear winter
After the impact of the meteorite that hypothetically caused the extinction of dinosaurs, the Earth was subjected to violent earthquakes and seaquakes, powerful winds, and acid rain. The impact caused columns of smoke and dust to rise to the upper atmosphere. The sky darkened, and the temperature fell dramatically, radically upsetting the climatic balance. The planet remained cold and dark for many years.

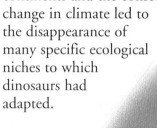

THE CATASTROPHE THEORY

In 1978, the American geologist Walter Alvarez made a discovery in the clay of the Scaglia Rossa, a succession of sedimentary rocks found in various places on the Earth's surface. He found that the clay had an abnormally high content of iridium, a chemical element that is very rare on Earth but which is present in asteroids. The stratum of red clay marks the geological boundary between the Cretaceous and the Paleocene and conserves clear signs of the extinction. Alvarez had thus found evidence in favor of his thesis that the disappearance of dinosaurs was caused by a meteorite. Subsequently, a crater where the impact was thought to have taken place was discovered off the Yucatan peninsula in Mexico.

The survivors
According to the meteorite theory, dinosaurs disappeared because they were unable to survive the tough "nuclear winter." The life forms that managed to survive these extreme conditions were organisms living in the ocean depths, plants resistant to the cold, and animals that weighed less than 55 pounds (25 kg) and were thus better able to tolerate temperature swings.

Large new mountain chains included the Sierra Nevada in California, the Rocky Mountains in the western United States, and the European Alps.

In the seas, plankton, consisting of algae and microscopic organisms, multiplied at an incredible rate. Some species of single-cell algae secreted a kind of spherical calcareous skeleton consisting of small, oval platelets called coccoliths. For millions of years, the abundant calcareous remains of these algae deposited on the seabed. When the sea level dropped at the end of the Cretaceous, these deposits formed immense blocks of chalky rocks along coasts. The most famous ones are the white cliffs of Dover in England.

Foraminifera, also equipped with a calcareous shell, gave rise to vast sedimentary mud deposits. Indeed, the Latin word *creta,* meaning "chalk," gives its name to the entire geological period. Other plankton components, such as sponges and radiolarians, developed siliceous spicules or shells. Their corpses accumulated on the ocean floor, resulting in chert beds.

Toward the end of the Cretaceous, the sea level began to drop rapidly and the continents reemerged. Animals and plants were ready to colonize the immense expanses of land. But then, once again, the Earth was struck by a major catastrophe. ▸▸

Polar dinosaurs
Fossil remains appear to show that some dinosaurs even adapted to living in very cold climates near the poles. These were generally small and almost certainly warm-blooded herbivores and carnivores.

THE FRONTIERS OF KNOWLEDGE

JURASSIC PARK

Science does not exclude the possibility of being able to use DNA to recreate a dinosaur or even a whole park of enormous Mesozoic reptiles, as presented in Steven Spielberg's movie Jurassic Park. *All this would be possible through cloning, a genetic engineering technique that can be used to reproduce millions of copies of determinate regions of DNA. However, a cloning project like this would require something that has not yet been found, namely, a fossil with organic tissue containing, almost intact, the precious genetic material. For now it only happens in movies.*

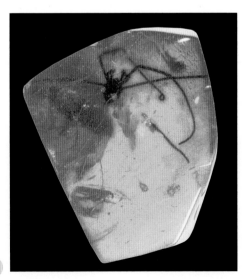

Birds

Not all dinosaurs became extinct. According to many scientists, today's birds are nothing other than the sole survivors of the evolutionary line of the terrible lizards. Some dinosaurs had already developed feathers and down to maintain body warmth; then, by chance, they managed to use these feathers to glide from tree to tree or to fly.

Archaeopteryx
Archaeopteryx had teeth, unlike present-day birds, and also had claws on its wings. These helped it to climb up tree trunks, just as an Amazonian bird called the hoazin does today. We do not know if *Archaeopteryx* was fully capable of flying or whether, apart from a few brief moments of flight, it basically glided.

Fossil feathers
The remains of *Archaeopteryx* are among the oldest fossils of birdlike reptiles. Uncovered for the first time in Germany in 1861, they date back at least 140 million years. In the best-preserved fossils left in the limestone, traces of feathers attached to the skeleton of a small dinosaur are clearly visible.

The history of Earth

Dying giants

About 65 million years ago something swept away 60% of all living species. We do not yet know for sure if there was just one cause, like the impact of a gigantic meteorite off the Mexican coast, or whether it was a combination of ecological and geological factors. We do know, however, that ichthyosaurs, mesosaurs, and plesiosaurs, together with half of all marine invertebrates (many foraminifera, echinoderms, mollusks, and all ammonites) disappeared from the oceans. In the air pterosaurs became extinct. On land many plants disappeared, as did all the dinosaurs, never to be seen again except in fossil form. All, that

is, except for one group, which survived and is still with us today. The descendants of certain dinosaurs, which had acquired feathers and learned to fly, survived the catastrophe. In fact, today's birds are probably the descendants of dinosaurs.

The catastrophe of the Cretaceous left the planet once again depopulated, but it opened the way for the evolution and expansion of a class of small beings that had remained on the sidelines for too long. They were small, furry, timid, nocturnal animals accustomed to living hidden away. But they were also very versatile and found a multitude of ecological niches to colonize. A new era, the Cenozoic, was about to dawn, and the stage was set for the triumph of mammals.

The development of wings

Fossil remains, organized in a genealogical tree of birds, show how wings probably developed from a flexible wrist used to capture fast-moving prey, as well as from the use of limbs to provide balance when running. Feathers, on the other hand, originally served to regulate body temperature.

MIGRATIONS

Zoologists are still amazed by the ability of many bird species to migrate immense distances. Experiments demonstrate that they use various sources of information to find their way: the Sun, the stars (some species recognize the Cassiopeia constellation or Little Bear), the Earth's magnetic field (which pigeons, for example, can perceive thanks to ferromagnetic particles in their beak). But it is still not clear how they manage to combine and use this information to calculate enormously long routes like those covered by the arctic tern, which travels from one pole to another.

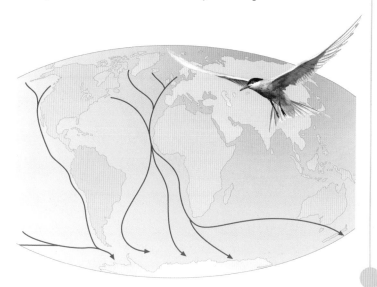

Toothed birds

Toothed birds became extinct during the Cretaceous. They mainly lived in coastal environments. *Ichthyornis* flew above the tops of the cliffs whereas *Hesperornis* had forgotten how to fly—like today's penguins, they hunted for fish by diving into the water and swimming.

Chapter 4
The triumph of mammals

Mammals had led a tough existence during the reign of the dinosaurs; now, in the desolate environment of the planet at the end of the Cretaceous, they put their experience to good use. In fact, the mammals of the time, which were no bigger than present-day mice, had become accustomed to a problem-filled nocturnal life in order to avoid the enormous predators roaming the planet. Thanks to this enforced survival course, they were well-placed to occupy the ecological niches left vacant after extinction of the dinosaurs.

Fur
Fur, which had already been developed by many reptiles in the Mesozoic, came to be of crucial importance for mammals in regulating body heat. Fur now allows mammals to live in widely diverse areas, from the Arctic to the deserts.

Koala

Kangaroo with young in her pouch

Duck-billed platypus

Egg or placenta?
The first mammals laid eggs, as the duck-billed platypus and echidna still do today. However, mammals subsequently perfected a mechanism allowing the mother to supply the embryo with nutrients and oxygen by means of a placenta and an umbilical cord, even though some fish, amphibians, and reptiles had already started to give birth to living young.

Wombat

Echidna

Dingo

Modern-day mammals
One of the places where the fabulous diversity of mammals can best be observed is Australia, where they can be found in water, on land, and in the air. There are marsupials, placentals, and even strange monotremes, namely, the duck-billed platypus and the echidna.

Binocular vision
At first mammals evolved as mainly nocturnal animals, with well-developed senses of sight and smell. The fact that their eyes were placed frontally, rather than on the sides of their heads, allowed most mammals to develop binocular vision, that is, the ability to perceive depth.

Numbat

Milk
Primitive mammals probably did not secrete milk, but mammary glands are now the characteristic that distinguishes this class of animals from all others. Milk is rich in fats and proteins, enabling newborn mammals to grow extremely rapidly. In their milk, mothers also pass on certain antibodies to their young.

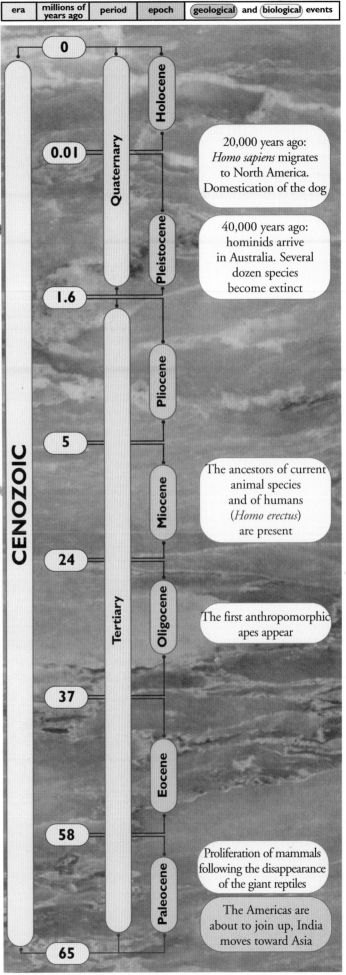

era	millions of years ago	period	epoch	geological and biological events
CENOZOIC	0	Quaternary	Holocene	
	0.01		Pleistocene	20,000 years ago: *Homo sapiens* migrates to North America. Domestication of the dog
	1.6			40,000 years ago: hominids arrive in Australia. Several dozen species become extinct
	5	Tertiary	Pliocene	
	24		Miocene	The ancestors of current animal species and of humans (*Homo erectus*) are present
	37		Oligocene	The first anthropomorphic apes appear
	58		Eocene	
	65		Paleocene	Proliferation of mammals following the disappearance of the giant reptiles. The Americas are about to join up, India moves toward Asia

Mammals and adaptive radiation

Mammals have proved capable of exploiting all the ecological niches vacated by the mass extinction in the Cretaceous. Some, like cetaceans, have developed forms similar to those of fish, whereas others, like bats, have transformed their feet into wings. They have even gone so far as to colonize extreme environments like the polar regions, which would have been virtually off-limits for the large reptiles of the past.

The genealogy of mammals

Fossil evidence indicates that all mammal groups derive from the same evolutionary line that started with cynodonts in the Triassic. Modern forms began to spread in the Cretaceous. Only monotremes have more ancient origins, as demonstrated by the fact that they continue to lay eggs.

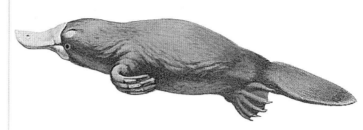

THE DUCK-BILLED PLATYPUS

In 1798, members of the Zoological Society in London first saw the hide of a strange aquatic mammal that had been found in Australia. Only after several years' discussion did the zoologists resign themselves to the idea that it was a rather special mammal with an anatomy that shared many reptile and bird characteristics. They baptized it Ornithorhynchus ("bird bill"). The only other member of the same order is the echidna, a kind of Australian porcupine that lays eggs and suckles its young.

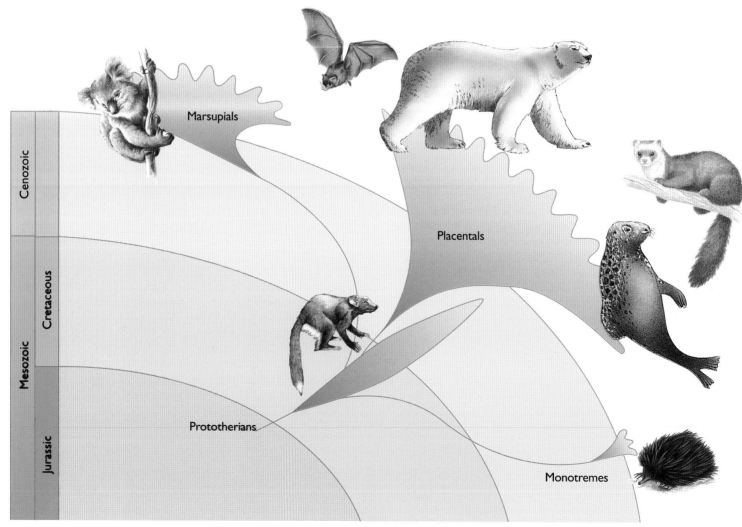

The development of mammals in the Cenozoic

Mammals were (and are) warm-blooded animals, an indispensable characteristic for adapting to highly diverse living environments. The ascent of mammals brings us to the Cenozoic era ("the era of recent history"), which began about 65 million years ago.

From a geological point of view, the planet assumed more or less the appearance it has today. Africa split away from South America and Australia. Some of today's highest mountain ranges were formed, including the Alps, the Pyrenees, the Himalayas, and the mountains of the Balkan peninsula.

The climate at the beginning of the Cenozoic was milder than it is today. In the first part of the Eocene, about 55 million years ago, the temperature rose, and it is considered the hottest epoch in the last 70–80 million years. Temperatures subsequently fell, the Earth became colder, and there were various glacial periods. Meanwhile, mammals diversified on all the continents and the tiny animals slowly grew in size. Three main branches developed. One resulted in marsupials, which include present-day kangaroos. Another branch led to the development of placentals, equipped with an internal organ in which the fetus develops. The final one, the most primitive and least common nowadays, comprised monotremes. ▶▶

CRYPTOZOOLOGY

This discipline studies animals whose existence is uncertain or legendary, such as the Loch Ness monster. One of the most celebrated of these is the yeti, the "abominable snowman"; it is almost certainly just a legend, but some people swear it is a large primate relative of humans that adapted to living in extreme mountain climates. Two biologists recently claimed to have discovered a mysterious clump of hair on a fence. DNA analysis apparently revealed that it belonged to an unknown mammal species.

From terrible lizards to terrible birds
During the Cenozoic, the niche once occupied by predatory biped dinosaurs was filled by gigantic birds. *Diatryma* (from the Greek, meaning "terrible crane"), which lived in North America 50 million years ago, was more than 6 feet (1.8 m) tall, had an enormous beak and hooklike claws. According to many experts, it fed on mammals up to the size of a small horse, chasing its prey on foot,

Messel: a complete ecosystem

The Messel pit, half an hour's drive from Frankfurt, Germany, is one of the most extraordinary fossil deposits in the world. The United Nations Educational, Scientific, and Cultural Organization (UNESCO) has declared it a world heritage site. By extracting more than 10,000 virtually intact plant and animal fossils, paleontologists were able to gain insight into an entire ecosystem, a community of interrelated living organisms dating back 49 million years.

The ecological cycle
The Messel fossils enable a detailed reconstruction of the ecological cycle of the time. The majority of living organisms belong to a cycle of the following kind: The sun's energy is trapped by plants in the form of sugars, which are then passed on to herbivores and finally to carnivores. Each organism consumes and gives off, in the form of heat, most of the energy it takes in with food; the rest is stored up. Finally, decomposers such as fungi and bacteria consume the remaining energy contained in dead tissue and release simple molecules, including carbon dioxide and water, which then reenter the cycle.

A tropical forest
About 50 million years ago the Messel lake, according to some experts, was surrounded by luxuriant tropical vegetation. As many as 65 plant species have been identified, including palms, grapes, and ferns.

Pangolin

In the trees
Many mammals adapted to living in trees. Often food remains have been found in their fossilized stomachs. Some fed on fruit, whereas others were predators. At Messel there were also pangolins, anteaters, many kinds of bats, and small horses with a taste for leaves and fruit.

Primate

Horse

Anteater

Python

Parental care and reproductive strategies

Reproduction is a complex issue for mammals as well as for other living creatures. One might think that if evolution rewards those beings that are best able to propagate their genes, that is, to produce the greatest number of descendants, the best strategy to adopt is to produce the highest possible number of seeds or embryos. But it does not always work like that because it is not enough just to reproduce: In order not to become extinct, the young must in turn grow and reproduce. For this reason, there are two types of reproductive strategies, in both the animal and the plant kingdoms.

Some animals and plants produce an enormous number of descendants, the strategy being that a few will survive to sexual maturity. Some plants produce thousands of seeds. Certain species of frogs and toads lay hundreds or thousands of eggs, and a female cod may produce 9 million in one year. The advantage of this strategy is obvious: The enormous number of offspring is such that, however hostile the environment and however many predators there may be, there is a good chance that a few will grow to maturity. But the disadvantage is that in producing so many embryos, the parents lack the energy to look after them and therefore have to leave them to fend for themselves. ▶▶

Conifers

Bat

Water lilies

Palms

WHERE WAS MESSEL?

Land, seawater, and freshwater animal remains have all been found at Messel. Many scientists have reached the conclusion that, about 50 million years ago, it must have been a lake, and that it was connected to the sea during some geological periods. But it is still an open issue that has all the makings of a minor paleontological mystery. If it was a tropical environment, as some people say, why, despite the discovery of many plants, are there no traces of tree trunks, bark, or roots? Why, if it was a lake, are there no aquatic insects like dragonflies and mosquitoes among numerous insect fossils?

Carnivores and herbivores

The Eocene ice age, about 37 million years ago, had important consequences for the spread of mammals, above all in Europe, where many species became extinct and were replaced by others from Asia. Besides the progenitors of modern-day felines, the Eocene and Oligocene (which lasted until about 23 million years ago) saw the appearance of big mammals and large numbers of herbivores. Some of these, taking advantage of the spread of pastureland, had learned to ruminate; that is, they had acquired the capacity to digest the cellulose contained in plants. Nonruminants were forced to expel this material, thereby wasting a substantial part of the food.

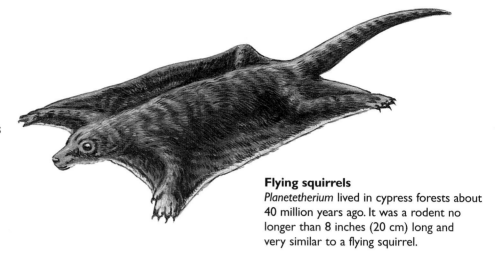

Flying squirrels
Planetetherium lived in cypress forests about 40 million years ago. It was a rodent no longer than 8 inches (20 cm) long and very similar to a flying squirrel.

Entelodont
With a prominent mane behind its neck, this animal invaded Europe from Asia. It was a giant warthog more than 6 feet (1.8 m) long.

Predatory mammals
Similar to a wolf, *Hyaenodon* was a creodont and one of the first carnivorous mammals. It spread across the planet more than 40 million years ago.

The history of the Earth

Other species, including mammals and birds, choose the opposite reproductive strategy. They generate few or very few offspring but devote lots of energy to them: supplying the egg with nutrients (or the seed, in the case of plants) or taking care of their young for a long time after birth, watching over them to ensure healthy growth. This strategy naturally guarantees a high survival rate. But an accident, an illness, or a particularly devastating attack by predators is all it takes to wipe out the fruits of an entire reproductive season.

On land and in the sea

Mammals did not only spread on land. The massacre of the late Cretaceous had not spared the oceans, and some mammals did not hesitate to take advantage of the vacant spaces.

About 50 million years ago, the ancestors of dolphins and whales retraced, in the opposite direction, the path taken by some vertebrates when they emerged from the oceans onto dry land about 250 million years previously. The transition back to the sea was a long process and required a good deal of adaptation. In the end, however, with the help of a few "tricks," like coming up to the surface every now and then for a breath of air, they managed to make the distinctive characteristics of their class compatible with life in water. ▶▶

The mammal giant
This animal was the biggest known terrestrial mammal. Standing 16 feet (4.8 m) tall at the shoulder, the Asian *Indricotherium* towered over all other creatures.

Brontotherium
Similar to a rhino, this giant of the Oligocene was 8 feet (2.4 m) tall at the shoulder, was 16 feet (4.8 m) long, and weighed 4.5 tons.

THE EXPANSION OF PRAIRIES

The herbaceous plants that now bend in the wind on prairies began to spread in the Cenozoic and are a product of the evolution of flowering plants. Theories to explain the expansion of these plants do not consider just climatic influences; some scientists argue that they developed continuously growing leaves in order to survive the attacks of herbivores.

Saber-toothed cats
These animals were the most fearsome enemies of *Indricotherium*. Despite their name, saber-toothed cats were not felines but belonged to various groups that have since become extinct. They were ferocious predators who used their "sabers" to savage prey. They probably did not kill their victim at once but waited for it to die from blood loss.

The early primates

Having taken to the trees in order to escape hazards on the ground, ancient primates, which resembled small rodents, acquired characteristics that made them ideal tree inhabitants capable of jumping, climbing, and running like acrobats in the thick vegetation. Distinctive characters included frontal eyes and a short snout; both features reflect the fact that for successful orientation among trees, good eyesight was more important than a developed sense of smell. Primates were initially insectivores but changed their dietary customs with time, learning to eat fruit and leaves as well.

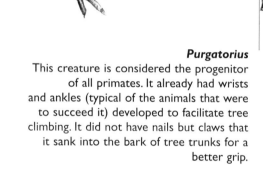

Purgatorius
This creature is considered the progenitor of all primates. It already had wrists and ankles (typical of the animals that were to succeed it) developed to facilitate tree climbing. It did not have nails but claws that it sank into the bark of tree trunks for a better grip.

STORIES AND PIONEERS OF SCIENCE

STRANGE LITTLE MEN OF MADAGASCAR

With their hybrid appearance and expressive gaze, lemurs have always appealed to the human imagination. Some species move among the trees at dawn and at dusk, emitting sharp cries to mark their territory. Early explorers were so frightened by them that they ascribed the voices to lemuri, *the ancient Romans' name for the wandering spirits of the dead. Lemurs also featured in numerous legends of Madagascar's native peoples; for example, the indris, the largest lemur species, is called* babakoto, *that is, "small man." The natives also believed that in order to decide whether or not to look after their young, the mother and father indris threw the baby from one to the other. If the baby fell, it was abandoned to its fate.*

While mammals were spreading on land and in the seas, climatic variations once again affected life on Earth. The planet became colder and colder. A first sharp drop in temperature took place between the Eocene and the Oligocene, about 37 million years ago. The climate also became progressively more arid. Forests shrank, giving way to vast grassland areas. Many primitive mammals became extinct as a result of these environmental changes, but new ones appeared in their place, including horses and other herbivores suited to feeding on low-growing vegetation. This period, also known as the age of the grasslands, lasted from 26 to about 7 million years ago and saw development of the majority of plant species known today.

The Miocene was marked by the appearance, on the plains, not only of creatures that would seem bizarre to us but also of many animals that might be taken for modern ones. Among the mammals spreading on Earth there were also primates—the most ancient progenitors of humans—the ultimate primates.

From the first primates to humans

Human beings, present-day apes, and all other primates probably descend from a small mammal that lived 70 million years ago in the forests of the late Cretaceous. ▶▶

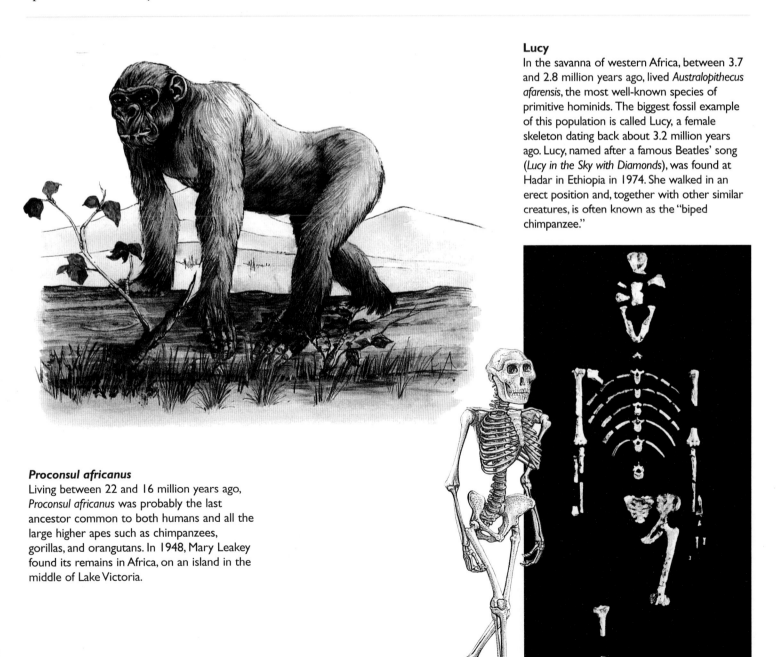

Proconsul africanus
Living between 22 and 16 million years ago, Proconsul africanus was probably the last ancestor common to both humans and all the large higher apes such as chimpanzees, gorillas, and orangutans. In 1948, Mary Leakey found its remains in Africa, on an island in the middle of Lake Victoria.

Lucy
In the savanna of western Africa, between 3.7 and 2.8 million years ago, lived Australopithecus afarensis, the most well-known species of primitive hominids. The biggest fossil example of this population is called Lucy, a female skeleton dating back about 3.2 million years ago. Lucy, named after a famous Beatles' song (Lucy in the Sky with Diamonds), was found at Hadar in Ethiopia in 1974. She walked in an erect position and, together with other similar creatures, is often known as the "biped chimpanzee."

The genus *Homo*

Homo sapiens has been the only living representative of its genus on Earth for about the last 35,000 years. Before, however, numerous species of hominid developed, coexisted, competed, and declined. Their coexistence in various periods of the Earth's history is proof that the evolution of our species was not a linear process of transformation from one species into another. *Homo sapiens* is not at the top of the evolutionary tree of hominids, merely the only small branch still alive. According to some scientists, the invention of language is what gave us such an enormous competitive advantage over our direct adversaries in the past.

Flat-faced *Homo*
Discovered and analyzed by paleontologist Meave Leakey in early 2001, the skull of *Kenyanthropus* ("flat-faced Kenyan hominid") may be that of a still unknown hominid, a direct ancestor of present-day humans. Dating back almost 3.5 million years, it is the oldest anthropoid skull ever found intact.

Coexistence
About 1.8 million years ago, at least four types of hominids shared the same environment. No one knows how they interacted, but around Lake Turkana, in northern Kenya, *Homo habilis, Homo ergaster, Homo rudolfensis,* and *Paranthropus bosei* all coexisted.

STORIES AND PIONEERS OF SCIENCE

THE PILTDOWN HOAX

In 1911, amateur paleontologist Charles Dawson claimed he had found the remains of a human skull at Piltdown in England. It was completely reassembled and studied over the years by many scientists. The robust teeth and the large, wide skull, capable of containing a sizable brain, led people to believe that a developed human ancestor had already existed in remote eras and that the skull dated to a period before Neanderthal man. This conviction lasted until 1953, when it emerged that it was all a hoax: The skull and jaw belonged respectively, to a present-day man and an anthropomorphic ape.

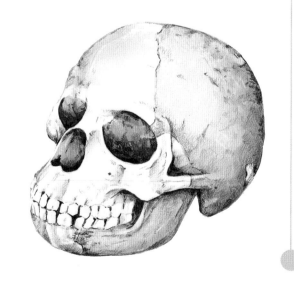

Human ancestors
The path from the first primate to modern humans is far from linear. From *Purgatorius*, various evolutionary lines developed with greater or lesser degrees of success. Humans represent, together with chimpanzees, orangutans, and other anthropomorphic apes, one of the most successful experiments to date.

THE FRONTIERS OF KNOWLEDGE

EVOLUTION AND THE BRAIN

In order to develop and function, especially at a young age, the brain requires a large proportion of the available resources. The brain of a newborn baby, despite being just 10% of body weight, consumes about 60% of the energy supplied by the mother's milk. This supply of energy in the form of milk is thought to have diminished in the last few millennia, resulting in a reduction in the size of the human brain. Contrary to what one might think, it seems that our species' brain has become smaller over the last 20,000 years.

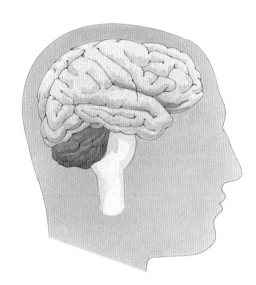

The history of Earth

The precursor of primates was *Purgatorius* (after Purgatory Hill, in the United States, where its remains were found); this animal resembled a squirrel and had taken to the trees to escape ground-level dangers. It seems incredible that this minute "forest acrobat" gave rise to *Homo sapiens*, which dominates the planet today. Yet it seems that this is precisely what happened. Reconstructing the phases of human evolution is not easy though, because there are many gaps in the fossil record. However, the general outline is now fairly clear. Immediately after the extinction of dinosaurs, descendants of *Purgatorius* differentiated into a large number of species and spread throughout Europe, Asia, and North America. From these ancestral primates descended the modern-day lemurs of Madagascar and the other prosimians (one of two primate suborders, the other being the apes) like the tarsier, which live in some areas of Africa and Southeast Asia. The first apes came on the scene about 30 million years ago. Compared to prosimians, they had more prehensile hands and feet (i.e., they were better at grabbing hold of branches and objects), were larger, and had a more developed brain. At the same time that apes were developing, Africa separated from America through tectonic plate movements. ▸▸

Out of Africa

According to the most accredited theory, our ancestors were born in Africa and spread from there throughout the rest of the world. This migration may have been caused by difficulties resulting from the climate. It is thought that dry periods in the African deserts left little available game for prehistoric hunting communities, so they were forced to look for food elsewhere, starting with the Middle East. From there, about 100,000 years ago, *Homo sapiens* apparently began its relentless colonization of the planet. The exact phases of this expansion remain uncertain, though. For example, there is considerable doubt about the number of species that evolved in Africa and when they really began to spread.

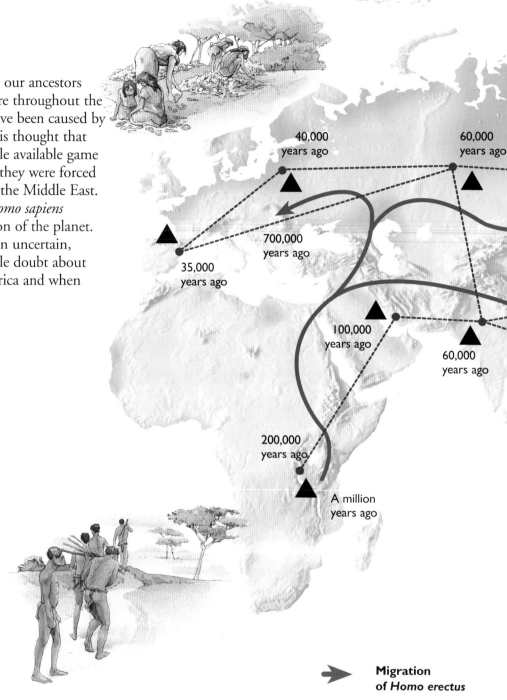

Multiregional theory

Besides the "Out of Africa" theory, there is another hypothesis about the origin of modern humans. According to what is known as the regional continuity theory, starting from *Homo erectus*, various populations developed in different regions of the world. These groups evolved independently but continued to exchange genes, finally resulting in *Homo sapiens*.

The first emigrants

The map compares the African and the multi-regional theories of the origin of modern *Homo sapiens*. Recent studies seem to support the former, but complications arise from new data, which suggest that successive waves of humans emigrated from Africa much earlier than was thought.

➡ **Migration of *Homo erectus***

▲ **Local populations of *Homo erectus* evolve toward *Homo sapiens* (multiregional hypothesis)**

–•– **Migration of *Homo sapiens* (African hypothesis)**

STORIES AND PIONEERS OF SCIENCE

THE FLOOD

In recent years many scholars have tried to work out what sort of event could have generated the myth of the Flood that exists in various parts of the world. Perhaps it was the memory of huge floods that occurred in Mesopotamia, or the rise in sea level after the end of a glacial period, or the flooding of the Black Sea area about 7,600 years ago.

25,000
years ago

50,000
years ago

A million
years ago

,000
ars ago

A million
years ago

60,000
years ago

50,000
years ago

40,000
years ago

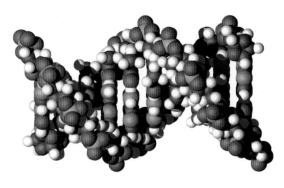

MITOCHONDRIAL DNA

Genetics has become one of the most effective modern means of answering the many unresolved questions of paleoanthropology. For instance, research into the origins of modern humans has benefited enormously from methods based on the analysis of mitochondrial DNA. This DNA is found in cell organelles called mitochondria. It is inherited from the mother and is subject to very slow mutations, all of which means that mitochondrial genes can be regarded as "molecular clocks." In fact, at least as far as maternal transmission is concerned, they provide an exact account of the genetic history of the organism.

The history of the Earth

Available remains seem to indicate that toward the Eocene-Oligocene, some primates evolved into two collateral branches, platyrrhines, ancestors of South American apes, and catarrhines, ancestors of African apes. Catarrhines split in turn into other branches. A member of one of these branches seems to have been *Ramapithecus*. This primate dates back 15 million years and for a long time was considered to be our oldest ancestor, though it now seems more likely that it belonged to a collateral branch of our genealogical tree. Very little is known about what happened between these early life forms and about 4 million years ago. There are lots of gaps in the recorded evidence, and experts are awaiting the discovery of new fossils to resolve a number of open issues.

The greatest uncertainty regards our direct predecessors in the period lasting until 3.6 million years ago, when *Ardipithecus ramidus* made its appearance. This primate was very similar to the chimpanzee and ranged over the vast savanna areas of eastern Africa. It already had a characteristic typical of the hominids that would soon spread across the planet: bipedalism. *Ardipithecus ramidus* had learned to walk upright. This ability became the distinctive feature of the first ancestors that we really do know well: australopithecines. ▸▸

Ice ages

On five occasions during the period in which we live, the Quaternary, ice has covered much of the land surface. These great decreases in temperature have always played an important role in the development of life. For instance, the ice ages may be one of the reasons why there are still many more ecological niches, and therefore species, in the tropics than in other latitudes. In fact, it is likely that in the regions not covered by ice, like the ones near the equator, life had plenty of time to diversify. In other regions, subjected to cold conditions at different moments in time, animals and plants were forced to move; they were able to recolonize the same zones only when the climate became milder again.

The signs of glaciation
An idea of the extent of glaciation in the past can be gained by considering the amount of material transported by glaciers. Long Island, for example, one of the neighborhoods of New York, consists of just one moraine.

STORIES AND PIONEERS OF SCIENCE

THE LAST ICE AGE

In the first half of the nineteenth century, the Swiss geologist Louis Agassiz was the first person to realize that in the past northern Europe had been covered by a thick layer of ice. At first elderly scholars did not believe him and even poked fun at his ideas. The scientific community's skepticism drove Agassiz to *climb previously unconquered mountain peaks in order to gather conclusive evidence that not only northern Europe but also much of England, Canada, and the northern United States had been covered by several miles of ice in the not too distant past.*

The history of the Earth

Australopithecine apes walked on their rear legs without having to lean on their knuckles, leaving their hands much freer to transport objects, to use tools, and to "clean" the carcasses left by lions and other predators. About 2.5 million years ago, a group of *Australopithecus africanus* finally gave rise to a human that was more similar to us than to a chimpanzee—*Homo habilis*, the first hominid to make effective stone chopping tools, which were used for various purposes. *Homo erectus* dates to 1.5 million years ago. He learned to light fires and build shelters. After *Homo erectus* came *Homo sapiens*, who probably managed to establish his species by successfully competing with the other hominid group that dominated Europe until 35,000 years ago: Neanderthal man, named after the Neander valley in Germany, where the first fossil remains were found in 1856.

Homo sapiens spread across the planet during the so-called Würm glaciation, the last of the five ice ages to have occurred in the Quaternary. The human species dealt with the severe climatic conditions that affected the planet until 10,000 years ago thanks to the development of an exclusive capacity: cultural adaptation. ▸▸

Moving glaciers
Pushed by the force of gravity, glaciers move downhill and, "scrape" the surrounding landscape like immense sheets of sandpaper. Traveling at a speed of about 6 feet (1.8 m) an hour, they leave numerous signs of their passage. One of these are moraines, deposits of the various materials that accumulate on the bottom and sides of the glaciers.

THE FRONTIERS OF KNOWLEDGE

THERMAL TRACES OF THE PAST

In order to find out what the mean temperatures were in different geological periods, and hence to build up a picture of the climate, researchers have come up with a number of paleothermometers. Two excellent indicators are the shape of plant leaves, which expand and contract according to whether it is hot or cold, and the abundance of oxygen isotopes in calcareous rocks.

The weapons of *Homo sapiens*

The last major period of glaciation, the Würm, was perhaps the most severe. It began 70,000 years ago and finished just 10,000 years ago, when Homo sapiens *already inhabited all the continents. At that time, ice fields covered the northern half of North America (at least as far as New York), much of Asia, and northern Europe as far south as the Alps. The human species spread in the final phase of the ice age. These early human beings probably managed to survive in very severe conditions thanks in part to their considerable mental abilities, which helped them develop elaborate hunting strategies.*

Early Europeans
They lived in groups and moved around in pursuit of game, their chief source of food.

Clothes
One of the secrets of *Homo sapiens'* success was the ability to make clothes by sewing together animal skins. Without the extraordinary invention of the needle, they would not have been able to deal with the cold.

Camps
Camps were rudimentary and easy to move. The huts had a frame of branches or large animal bones, which was then covered with skins. There were very few "household goods," but there was already the habit of collecting precious objects such as teeth or shells, which were also used for bartering.

Hunters
In the last glacial period, *Homo sapiens* killed large animals with spears or by laying traps for them on the ground. Smaller game was captured in nets.

The development of farming

Agriculture first developed in western Asia between 11,000 and 9,000 years ago. It then spread to, or was discovered independently in, many parts of the world. Many peoples switched from nomadic hunting and gathering to become sedentary crop growers and livestock breeders. This was probably the greatest technological and social revolution humanity has ever known. It permitted an enormous increase in the production of food per unit of occupied land and led to the birth of the first cities. However, the human impact on the environment increased drastically.

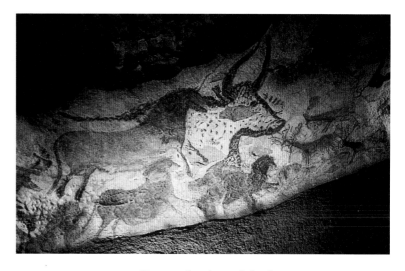

Domestication of the horse
The archaeological data are not conclusive, but it seems that the horse, which had been hunted by humans since very early times, was first domesticated on the steppes between Ukraine and Mongolia about 5,000 years ago.

THE FRONTIERS OF KNOWLEDGE

DIET AND EVOLUTION

The use of tools and the development of a social organization undoubtedly favored the growth of human cognitive capacities. One of the factors that contributed to the evolution of the brain was food. Early humans had a partly carnivorous diet, which was based not only on hunting but also on the scavenging of carcasses; this kind of activity was greatly facilitated by the ability to use stone tools to break bones and cut flesh. Social cooperation was also very important in procuring meat.

The history of the Earth

The achievements of *Homo sapiens*

Homo sapiens had learned to wear the skins of other animals as protection against the cold, had learned to light fires for warmth and protection against predators, and had begun to pass on acquired knowledge from one generation to the next. These are all aspects of a human culture that developed in various ways in different parts of the world according to geographic conditions. The earliest human communities were nomadic and based on hunting and gathering. About 10,000 years ago, humans also began to produce food by cultivation. Agriculture developed in various parts of the world, leading to the establishment of permanent settlements,

the founding of the first cities, and a progressive subdivision of labor. From this moment onward, the signs of human presence on the planet became increasingly evident, and the history of the Earth became more and more bound up with that of humans. The industrial revolution of the nineteenth century and the present-day technological revolution are just two of the most obvious steps in the ongoing transformation of the environment, which humans have conditioned and accelerated in a quite unprecedented way. The consequences and contradictions of this activity are reflected in the world today.

Why did agriculture develop?

Until recently it was thought that agriculture spread rapidly because it represented a great step forward in comparison to hunting and gathering. But some scholars now maintain the exact opposite. They argue that overpopulation and the reduction in available resources forced some populations to think up the agricultural system despite the fact that it was labor-intensive and thus unappealing from a quality-of-life point of view.

The first human-related extinctions

Primitive hunters were highly skilled. According to many experts, the extinction of some large American mammals occurred at the same time as the first human migrations and was the result of hunting. The best-known victims were the mastodon, the mammoth, and the giant sloth (above).

PALEOLITHIC "VENUSES"

Interpretation of the numerous Paleolithic and Neolithic statues depicting female bodies has always been controversial.
In the nineteenth century, Johann Jakob Bachofen, basing his theory partly on these "Venuses," hypothesized that many past civilizations were matriarchal, that is, dominated by women. His thesis has now been largely discredited, but some archaeologists believe that the birth of the great sedentary communities, based on agriculture and the defense of goods, favored development of the notion of private property and social models based on a "warrior" male and a dependent female. The debate is still very heated.

Chapter 5
Humans and the planet

The Holocene, the epoch we live in and the most recent phase in the history of the Earth, has been very brief. Just a few thousand years have elapsed since humans first started growing crops and rearing livestock. This is no time at all when compared to the planet's age of 5 billion years—a mere instant in relation to the slow pace of geology and natural evolution. Yet the world has changed greatly since the beginning of the Holocene. Not so much because of plate tectonics, mutations, or the pressure of natural selection, but mainly as a result of *Homo sapiens*, the sole living species capable of radically modifying the environment.

Looking after rivers, woods, and hills
When modifying a given area, one must consider hydrogeological factors. Ill-conceived buildings, damming, and deforestation can all create the conditions that lead to landslides.

Artificial selection
Humans use the basic mechanisms of evolution to modify other living species—for example, domestic animals and fruit trees—to their advantage. Country dwellers and breeders have known about this for centuries. Instead of allowing natural selection to take its course, artificial selection is adopted to ensure that only individuals with useful characteristics reproduce.

Emigrating to the city
Many species, although they have not become domesticated, have adapted to life in towns and cities, feeding on garbage and exploiting the new climatic and ecological conditions that have developed.

Defense against earthquakes
Unable to prevent earthquakes from happening, humans have developed antiseismic construction techniques.

New materials
Oil and materials synthesized by humans have many applications, but overuse causes serious ecological imbalances.

An extra environment

Besides the large natural environments, modern cities represent a new human-made "habitat." But cities are not just polluted places inhabited by humans. Many organisms, ranging from rooftop lichens to birds of prey, insects, migrating birds, amphibians, and reptiles live and reproduce in urban areas.

Dangerous aliens?

The introduction of nonnative species (such as the gray squirrel in many European cities and parks) is one of the chief causes of extinctions. Biodiversity is currently going through one of its toughest periods.

period	events
1999	Human population: 6 billion
1985	Dramatic increase in the hole in the ozone layer. International environmental treaties
1975	Human population: 4 billion
1970	Discovery of a hole in the ozone layer
1950–2000	Large-scale deforestation, mass extinctions, international projects to safeguard biodiversity. The greenhouse effect grows and becomes a global problem
1930	Human population: 2 billion
1909	First European national park set up in Sweden
1871–72	Establishment of Yellowstone National Park, the first national park in the world
1825–50	Human population reaches 1 billion
1750–1800	Industrial revolution. Intensive deforestation to build railways, produce charcoal, etc. Human population increases. CO_2 emissions and beginnings of the greenhouse effect
1400–1600	Invention of printing; scientific revolution
Eleventh century	Acceleration in population growth
3,500–2,000 years ago	Iron Age
5,000–3,500 years ago	Bronze Age
6,000–5,000 years ago	Founding of the first cities in Mesopotamia
12,000–11,000 years ago	Neolithic revolution in Mesopotamia; increase in the amount of available food and the beginning of deforestation. Population growth. Domestication of many animals

Small but skilled

Despite the success of humans, small creatures like insects and microorganisms are and will continue to be the real dominators of the planet.

The biosphere and biodiversity

The only known place in the universe where life forms exist is the biosphere, a layer of water, air, and earth about 12 miles (20 km) thick. This layer is very thin in comparison to the overall diameter of the Earth—more than 7,200 miles (12,000 km)—but sufficient to host an incredible variety of life forms. It has become clear in the last few decades that this biodiversity is of fundamental importance for our survival.

The biosphere
The biosphere stretches from the upper atmosphere—about 31,500 feet (9,700 m) above sea level—where only a small number of insects and microorganisms can survive, to the maximum depth of the ocean abysses, about 35,750 feet (11,000 m) below sea level, inhabited by a few organisms capable of decomposing organic matter sinking down from above.

STORIES AND PIONEERS OF SCIENCE

THE GREAT FAMINE IN IRELAND

The Great Famine, which struck Ireland between 1846 and 1850, caused the death, through starvation, of 1,250,000 people and produced almost 2 million refugees. It was caused by the spread of a parasite fungus which completely destroyed most of the potato crop for five consecutive years. The Great Famine can be seen as a warning of the need to preserve biodiversity. If there had been many different varieties and if the population's diet had not been based almost exclusively on potatoes, the tragedy could have been avoided.

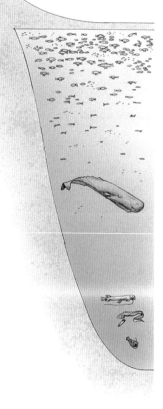

The history of the Earth

An animal with a thousand habitats

Many organisms are able to modify the environment in which they live. Some species of plants and trees release chemical substances into the ground through their roots that inhibit or encourage the presence of other species. Coral polyps construct immense reefs that provide habitats for other organisms. Bees, termites, and ants build miniature "cities" based on complex, effective designs, inhabited by tens of thousands of individuals organized in a rigorous social structure. Beavers construct dams capable of altering the course of streams, thereby creating artificial microenvironments. However, the human species is the only one capable of exploiting the characteristics of the surrounding environment so ably and of altering it so radically that it is possible to inhabit every corner of the planet—from the rainforests to the highest mountains, from the deserts to the polar ice sheets.

Human activity has left deep and indelible marks on the environment. The composition of the terrestrial atmosphere, the water of rivers and oceans, and even the ice fields of the Antarctic, bear unequivocal traces of our presence. We are even visible from outside the planet. When the Earth is observed at night from an artificial satellite, human activity is clearer than ever: Thousands of yellow and white lights signal the position of our cities, hundreds of red dots indicate the presence of oil wells and the fires we light in forests or grasslands. ▸▸

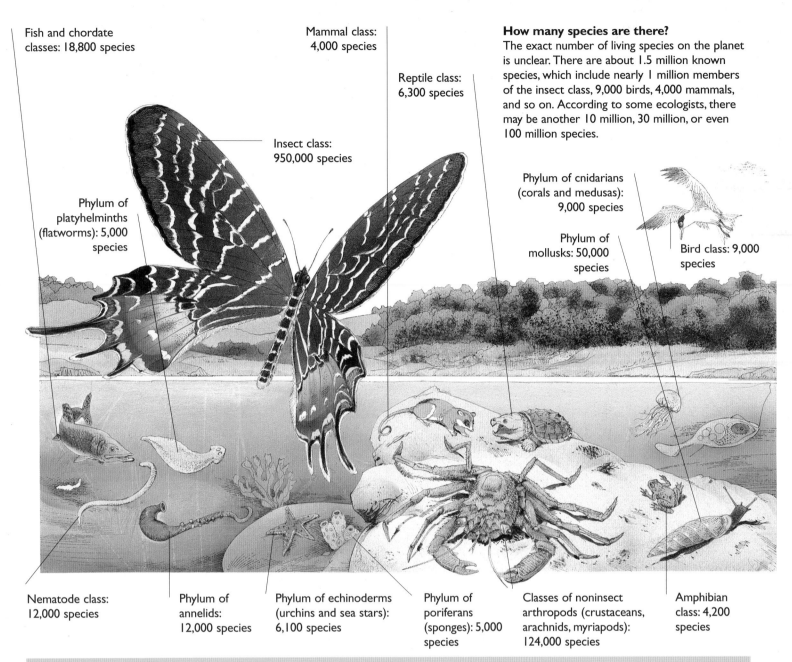

Fish and chordate classes: 18,800 species

Mammal class: 4,000 species

Reptile class: 6,300 species

How many species are there?
The exact number of living species on the planet is unclear. There are about 1.5 million known species, which include nearly 1 million members of the insect class, 9,000 birds, 4,000 mammals, and so on. According to some ecologists, there may be another 10 million, 30 million, or even 100 million species.

Insect class: 950,000 species

Phylum of platyhelminths (flatworms): 5,000 species

Phylum of cnidarians (corals and medusas): 9,000 species

Phylum of mollusks: 50,000 species

Bird class: 9,000 species

Nematode class: 12,000 species

Phylum of annelids: 12,000 species

Phylum of echinoderms (urchins and sea stars): 6,100 species

Phylum of poriferans (sponges): 5,000 species

Classes of noninsect arthropods (crustaceans, arachnids, myriapods): 124,000 species

Amphibian class: 4,200 species

THE FRONTIERS OF KNOWLEDGE

BIODIVERSITY HOT SPOTS

In 1988, the English ecologist Norman Myers proposed a number of criteria for identifying the most biodiverse areas in the world, which he called "biodiversity hot spots." One of his key parameters was the number of endemic species present, that is, species that do not live anywhere else. The most important hot spots are in Madagascar, the Philippines, Borneo, the eastern coast of Brazil, and the Caribbean. These are all high-risk habitats, given that more than 90% of their overall area has already been destroyed.

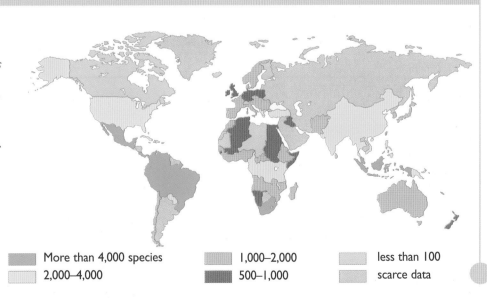

More than 4,000 species

2,000–4,000

1,000–2,000

500–1,000

less than 100

scarce data

The cycles of the biosphere

The matter that we and all other living beings are made of is in constant movement. It is transferred from one organism to another or to the ground, atmosphere, or water through respiration, digestion, and decomposition. Gigantic cycles of matter involve a global movement of water, carbon, and mineral salts.

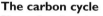

The carbon cycle

Plants absorb carbon dioxide from the atmosphere and use it to produce sugars by means of photosynthesis. However, they immediately return some of this carbon dioxide through respiration. Animals absorb carbon from the plants they eat. They use some of it for body tissue and release some into the atmosphere, through respiration, in the form of carbon dioxide. Fungi, bacteria, and other decomposers feed on sewage or dead organisms and return some carbon to the atmosphere, also in the form of carbon dioxide.

The history of the Earth

Besides shaping natural environments for their own purposes, humans are also capable of constructing large artificial ecosystems. Cities and monocultural farming systems are the most evident examples.

Life in the city

A city is not just a collection of houses and buildings. It contains fully fledged ecosystems, in other words, basic ecological units formed by communities of organisms bound together by complex exchanges of matter and energy. Cities are not populated only by humans and the species they brought with them (cockroaches, mice, rats, etc.). Rooftops are often covered by lichens, some of which provide a useful indication of the amount of pollution in the air and rainwater. Roadsides, lawns, and walls are colonized by mosses or small herbaceous plants, grasses and nettles for instance, which host invertebrates and provide food for the caterpillars of some butterfly species. There is no lack of amphibians or reptiles: Lizards and geckos (in cities with a hot or temperate climate) feed on the numerous insects they find on terraces or in gardens, and public parks often play host, near fountains or in ponds, to toads, frogs, and tree frogs and sometimes to green lizards, tortoises, and small snakes. Birds are also unvaryingly present in major urban settlements. Gulls, for instance, have adapted to searching for food in city refuse dumps, often choosing to spend the night there as well. ▶▶

The mineral cycle in oceans

Mineral salts, of which land masses have a plentiful supply, are dissolved and carried into the sea by river currents. Once there, they are absorbed by the microorganisms comprising phytoplankton and transferred to fish, whales, and other animals that feed on it. When these animals die and decompose, the salts precipitate into the seabeds; some of them reenter the cycle thanks to thermal currents, and others pass into seabirds or humans who feed on marine animals.

The water cycle

Every day an average of 660 million cubic yards (500 m³) of water enters the atmosphere, and a similar amount returns to the land. Water in seas, rivers, and lakes evaporates in the Sun, with some of the vapor rising into the atmosphere until it condenses into clouds. Some of the water that falls as rain, snow, or hail flows, underground or on the surface, to the sea, participating in the cycle. Some is absorbed by plants, animals, and other living beings and then emitted again in the form of water vapor through transpiration, sweating, respiration, or combustion.

RELEASE OF CARBON DIOXIDE (CO₂)

Areas where peat (the first stage in the formation of coal) accumulates are called peat bogs; they are found prevalently in cold regions like northern Europe, Siberia, and Alaska. Large quantities of carbon dioxide form, but it is not emitted into the atmosphere because of a surface layer of ice. According to some research, however, this natural trap could prove ineffective if the planet, as seems to be happening, continues to become warmer. The ice sheets might melt, releasing the enormous quantities of carbon dioxide currently imprisoned in the peat.

97

The major natural environments

The structure of the ecological niches of an environment, and hence the type of organisms that can live there, depend crucially on the climate and the chemical composition of the terrain. If two geographically distant areas have the same kind of environmental characteristics, it is likely that they will develop ecosystems belonging to the same basic type. These types are called biomes. Two ecosystems belonging to the same biome have similar ecological niches; evolution will lead to the appearance of species that are sometimes similar in structure, physiology, or behavior despite the fact that they are unrelated.

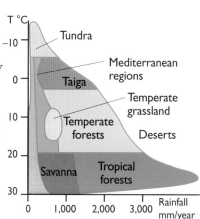

Biomes and climate
The two most important climatic factors in determining the type of biome that will form in a given geographic area are temperature and rainfall. Deserts, as can be seen in the graph, may be in very hot or very cold areas and are characterized by a scarcity of rainfall. In hot regions, differences in rainfall are what determine whether an area will be occupied by savanna or tropical forest.

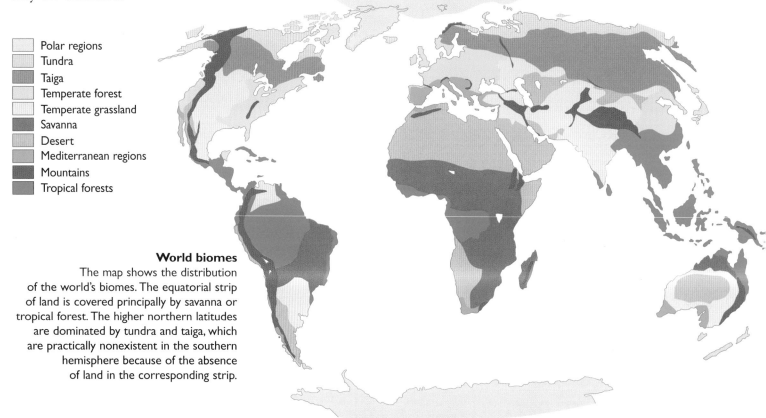

- Polar regions
- Tundra
- Taiga
- Temperate forest
- Temperate grassland
- Savanna
- Desert
- Mediterranean regions
- Mountains
- Tropical forests

World biomes
The map shows the distribution of the world's biomes. The equatorial strip of land is covered principally by savanna or tropical forest. The higher northern latitudes are dominated by tundra and taiga, which are practically nonexistent in the southern hemisphere because of the absence of land in the corresponding strip.

THE FRONTIERS OF KNOWLEDGE

THE BIOSPHERE EXPERIMENT

Various experiments are underway to try to understand more about how a small, closed ecosystem functions and whether it is self-sufficient. The most famous experiments are the small-scale ones conducted on orbiting space stations, and Biosphere 2, a sealed construction in the Arizona desert. It covers an area of less than 5 acres and has a volume of 270,000 cubic yards (204 m³). It is inhabited by a few humans who are trying to live and remain self-sufficient in one or more of the miniature ecosystems.

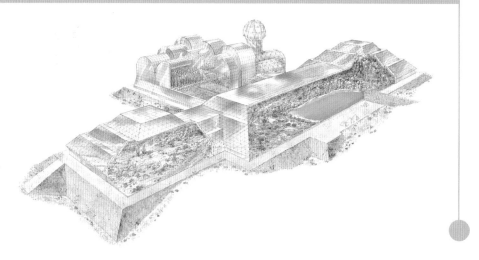

Pigeons and turtledoves proliferate on the roofs of old buildings. In some cities, starlings opt to spend the winter months amid the avenues and buildings. The average temperature in cities is higher, there are no hunters, predators are less numerous than in the countryside, and there is no shortage of food. Swallows, house martins, sparrows, tits, jackdaws, and crows may also spend some or all of their lives in the city.

At the top of the food pyramid are various ranks of predators: Foxes are frequent visitors to suburban gardens and meadows, and birds of prey such as the kestrel, peregrine falcon, and owl nest in some cities, feeding on lizards, geckos, rodents, and small birds.

Environments

In places that are geographically distant but have similar environmental features (rainfall, soil composition, average temperature, etc.), similar ecosystems evolve with equivalent ecological niches. For example, in areas where herbaceous vegetation dominates, medium- and large-sized herbivores evolve; they live in herds as a defense against predators. Sometimes similar niches are occupied by organisms that resemble each other because they have to exploit similar resources. This phenomenon is called adaptive convergence and has led, for example, to the evolution of two similar large birds, the ostrich and the moa (now extinct), one in Africa and the other in Oceania. ▸▸

Polar regions

Tundra

STORIES AND PIONEERS OF SCIENCE

KROPOTKIN'S MUTUAL AID THEORY

The Russian prince, naturalist, and geographer Piotr Kropotkin (1842–1921) was one of the pioneers of anarchist thinking. Studying the Siberian ecosystem, he became convinced that, despite competition between species, evolutionary success within a species was assured not by no-holds-barred conflict but thanks to cooperation and mutual aid. We now know that cooperation is very common in nature and that evolution has led to the appearance of numerous stratagems to offset conflict between members of the same species.

Taiga

Temperate forests

Mediterranean regions

Mountains

Temperate grasslands

Savannas

Tropical forests

Deserts

Polar regions

In polar regions the sun shines, low above the horizon, for just a few months each year. Cold and darkness prevail for the rest of the time. Plants cannot live in these environments, where winter temperatures are way below freezing. Yet in the summer even polar regions teem with life. Abundant plankton forms the basis for a complex food chain that includes numerous species of fish, birds, and mammals.

STORIES AND PIONEERS OF SCIENCE

AMUNDSEN'S EXPEDITION

The Norwegian explorer Roald Amundsen (1872–1928) decided when he was still a child that he wanted to reach the poles. At the age of 21, he abandoned medical studies to dedicate himself to exploration. On December 14, 1911, he and his companions beat the Englishman Robert Scott in the race to become the first people to reach the South Pole. Amundsen died in an air crash during a rescue mission to the North Pole to save a group led by the Italian explorer Umberto Nobile. His body was never found.

The Antarctic

The Antarctic interior is inhabited almost exclusively by microorganisms. However, near the coasts there are various species of penguins, as well as seals, orcas, albatrosses, skuas, blue whales, and sea elephants.

Many small woodland animals incapable of rapid flight have evolved defensive quills. The Australian echidna is very similar to the porcupine despite the fact that they are entirely unrelated.

Let's look at the main biomes, that is, types of environment, on our planet. The polar regions are covered by a permanent cap of ice. Inland there are very few life forms, and these consist almost exclusively of microorganisms. But various animal species live near the water, especially in the summer when the ice pack breaks up. Species include large mammals and birds that have adapted to the harsh ecosystem by developing insulating feathers, thick layers of fat, or small, barely

protruding corporeal appendages. The purpose of these is to preserve body heat.

The tundra lies south of the polar ice cap, at lower latitudes. Average temperatures are 14°F (–10°C). Rainfall is scarce, about the same as in the areas bordering the Sahara desert. Water is present in liquid form only during the summer. This, together with strong winds, has meant that only herbaceous plants or small, twisted trees have managed to evolve. One of these is the Arctic willow, which grows with its trunk almost flat along the ground. However, in the summer the tundra teems with life. Days are extremely long, and temperatures are about 41°F (5°C). ▸▸

The Arctic
Whereas the South Pole is part of a large continent, with gigantic valleys and mountains, the arctic cap consists exclusively of ice floating on the sea, and the only land mass is Greenland. Herrings, whales, polar bears, seals, and walruses live on the ice and/or in the water.

THE FRONTIERS OF KNOWLEDGE

LIVING IN THE ANTARCTIC

Life at a scientific research station in the Antarctic is difficult. Paradoxically, the extreme cold means the air contains virtually no water vapor, and this makes the risk of fires very high. Falling ill is dangerous because bases can remain cut off for months. But you are unlikely to catch a cold. Given the outside temperature, few pathogenic bacteria can survive.

The northern forests

The taiga, or boreal forest, covers about 14 million square miles (more than 23 million square kilometers) of northern Europe, Asia, and North America. The trees in the taiga have adapted to survive in the cold, dry winters. Their needle-shaped leaves have very small surfaces, which minimize water loss. The majority of animals survive by going into hibernation or migrating southward.

Bald eagle
This bird is the symbol of the United States, but like many other animals at the top of the food pyramid, it is in serious risk of extinction. It is threatened by the disappearance of habitats and by pesticides, which accumulate in the fish, rodents, and small birds on which it feeds.

Elk
During the mating season, male elks engage in spectacular bouts of combat. They then shed their antlers, an awkward encumbrance when moving around in the vegetation.

Douglas fir
This imposing conifer can reach almost 300 feet (90 m) in height. In North America it is used as a Christmas tree and, above all, as a source of timber.

The history of the Earth

Around the pools that form in the tundra during the summer, there are swarms of insects, which attract birds. Mosses, lichens, and berry- and seed-producing plants attract hares, lemmings, reindeers, and musk oxen (or their North American ecological equivalent, caribous). Situated at the top of the food chain are small- and medium-sized carnivores, including owls, stoats, snowy owls, polar wolves, and wolves. The next biome, moving in the direction of the equator, is the taiga. This region is also very cold in winter but has a long, humid summer that enables the growth of conifer forests (pines, larches, firs, etc.). Conifer needles are chewed by red ants, which use them to build nests, and then decomposed by microorganisms, thereby allowing mineral salts to return to the ground.

There is greater biodiversity in the taiga than in the tundra because the variety of plants and the mild temperatures permit the existence of numerous ecological niches. Especially in the summer, conifers host many species of mammals and birds. Lemmings, squirrels, and field mice feed on seeds and berries. Nutcrackers and jays have powerful beaks with which they open up cones and eat the seeds. Bullfinches on the other hand, feed on new shoots and seeds, whereas grouse and mountain francolin make do with those that have fallen to the ground. Predators include sables, bears, lynxes, martens, wolves, and various birds of prey. ▸▸

THE DESTRUCTION OF THE TUNGUSKA FOREST

In 1908, a gigantic ball of fire lit up the Siberian skies in an uninhabited area called Tunguska. It was probably caused by a big meteorite hitting the ground with the energy of an atomic bomb a thousand times more powerful than the one used at Hiroshima. It completely destroyed hundreds of square miles of forest. More than 90 years later, the effects of that devastating impact can still be seen.

Red lynx
This agile feline chases squirrels and raids bird nests. It is capable of climbing the tallest and thinnest of tree branches.

Salmon
Salmon are born in fresh waters and then move to sea. They return to the river they were born in to reproduce, swimming upstream against the current. During the reproductive period they stop eating and almost always die soon afterward.

THE FRONTIERS OF KNOWLEDGE

ACID RAIN

Over the last few decades, highly acidic rain has caused enormous damage to forests around the world. The responsibility lies with pollutants emitted into the atmosphere. These include sulfur dioxide (SO_2), mainly produced by the combustion of oil and coal, and nitrogen oxides, contained in car exhaust fumes. When these substances dissolve in water, they are transformed into sulfuric and nitric acids.

Mediterranean environments

Near the sea the climate is very different from what it is like inland. The winters are mild, the summers hot and arid. Many plants, to minimize transpiration, have developed small, leathery leaves covered with a waxy film.

Many animals avoid the heat by emerging from their dens only at night or at dawn. Once very extensive, Mediterranean shrub land has shrunk considerably.

ARISTOTLE AND THE CLASSIFICATION OF LIVING BEINGS

Aristotle, the celebrated Greek philosopher who lived in the fourth century BC, was also an expert on Mediterranean fauna. He was one of the first people to attempt a classification, and he invented new words to denote certain groups of animals. For example, the word "coleopteran" derives from a Greek word of his invention.

Ilex and cork
These two robust, evergreen trees belong to the oak family. Cork bark has been exploited by humans since ancient times.

Mouflon
The Mouflon feeds on tubers, roots, and grasses. It is about 30 inches (75 cm) tall, and the adult male has large, curved horns. A skilled climber, it not only lives in Mediterranean environments but has also ventured into mountain areas.

Bonelli's eagle
Bonelli's eagle was once common to much of the Mediterranean, region, but it is very rare nowadays because of poaching and the deterioration of its habitat. It makes plunging dives to capture its prey of rodents and other small animals.

Several thousand years ago, the land to the south of the taiga and some areas to the north of the cold regions of the southern hemisphere were covered by massive temperate forests. Increased rainfall and the temperate climate enabled the growth of large trees with wide leaves. These forests are more fertile as well and consequently have been heavily colonized by humans. Only a small proportion of these large forests still remain almost all of which have been profoundly shaped by centuries of human presence. This prevents the development of climax ecosystems with an ultimate, dynamic, structural balance (generally characterized by considerable biodiversity).

Temperate forests are dominated by large trees such as oaks, beeches, and birches, which lose their leaves and scale down activity during winter. The massive quantity of dry fallen leaves is broken down and transformed into natural fertilizer by earthworms, insects, and microorganisms. Tree seeds can grow only in the clearing created by a fallen tree. The first saplings to become adult occupy the space and crowd out the others. In fact, beneath the treetops light is scarce and is sufficient to allow only ferns, mosses, and small flowering plants to grow.

Near the coasts, many temperate forests give way to another important biome, which has also shrunk considerably: Mediterranean shrubland and woodland. ▶▶

Wildcat
This animal is not a cat that has become wild but a species in its own right, a skilled predator found in Mediterranean woods and shrub land. They are now rare and are suspicious of humans. As it is difficult to observe them, zoologists seeking to map their presence often resort to playing recordings of the sounds made by the male. The real ones in the woods respond furiously to defend their territory.

Strawberry tree
The strawberry tree is one of the most characteristic bushes of Mediterranean vegetation. Its large, red fruit is edible.

THE FRONTIERS OF KNOWLEDGE

THE PROBLEM OF EROSION

The construction of roads and houses too close to the sea, combined with intensive tourism, often result in alteration of the vegetation and sea dunes. The disappearance of the colonizing plants that live on the beach is immediately accompanied by dune erosion. Sand is blown inland, where it gradually kills the shrub vegetation, which in turn causes erosion of the surrounding area. At least 70% of the dunes of the western Mediterranean region have already disappeared.

Savannas and grasslands

Savannas and grasslands once occupied vast areas, much of which have now been transformed into fields for crops or pastures for cattle. Many of the typical organisms of these ecosystems have been significantly reduced in number and face extinction.

Hyena
Hyenas live in groups led by a female. They mainly feed on carrion but are also skilled nocturnal predators.

Gnu
Like zebras and Thompson's gazelles, gnus migrate long distances to find the best pastures.

Lion
Despite what is commonly believed, lions are not particularly efficient predators. They hunt in groups, making short chases, and often steal prey killed by hyenas, African hunting dogs, and cheetahs.

STORIES AND PIONEERS OF SCIENCE

THE LEAKEY FAMILY

For decades the African savanna has been the stage for a series of discoveries by the Leakey family, an extraordinary dynasty of paleoanthropologists. They have found some of the most important human fossil remains. Louis Leakey was one of the first to demonstrate that the genus Homo originated in eastern Africa. In 1959, near Olduvai in Tanzania, his wife Mary found the remains of a hominid 1.75 million years old. And in 1978, at Laetoli, she discovered tracks in volcanic ash left by hominids 3.5 million years ago. Her son Richard and his wife Meave still conduct successful digs in Kenya. They have already found hominids dating back more than 4 million years.

Predators in the sky
Birds of prey are typical inhabitants of the grasslands and savanna. The large, open spaces are ideal for their hunting sessions.

DESERTIFICATION OF GRASSLANDS

Hundreds of thousands of square miles of grassland in China, South America, Africa, and Australia have been reduced to desert. This is an extremely serious phenomenon and is occurring on an even greater scale than deforestation. In Brazil and Argentina, 80% of grasslands and savannas have disappeared as a result of intensive cattle farming or soy plantations. Overexploitation of water and plant resources rapidly lead to impoverishment and erosion of the soil. However, in certain cases, the process of desertification can be reversed, provided steps are taken to reforest, to prevent the grazing of large animals, and to block the movement of sand dunes.

The history of the Earth

Mediterranean shrubland and woodland, despite the name, extend not only along the Mediterranean coasts, but also run along the coasts of California, western Australia, Chile, and the Cape of Good Hope.
Typical Mediterranean vegetation, consisting of shrubs and short trees, and the temperate environments are rich in animal and plant life.
However, the real triumph of global biodiversity is to be found in tropical forests. A single acre of forest on the Atlantic coast of Brazil or in the Andean rainforest contains hundreds of species of trees and thousands of species of invertebrates, many of which have yet to be studied or even identified.

The reason for the biological abundance of tropical forests is not entirely clear, but the constant climatic conditions are a determinant factor. Near the equator there are about 12 daylight hours throughout the year. It rains almost every day, and the daytime and nighttime and winter and summer temperatures do not vary much. Consequently, plants grow all the time, forming an ecosystem packed with exploitable ecological niches.
The tropical forest ecosystem is structured in layers. The upper layer comprises the treetops of the tallest trees, which reach heights of 160–190 feet (48–57 m).
▶▶

The tropical forests

Tropical forests currently cover less than 6% of the world's land surface. Yet according to many ecologists, they play host to between 50% and 60% of all living plant and animal species. Unfortunately, besides being the most biodiverse ecosystems, they are also the ones most threatened. In India, Sri Lanka, Bangladesh, and Haiti, practically all the virgin forests have disappeared. In the Philippines and Thailand, less than half remain. Along the Brazilian coast the figure is less than 5%, and at least 12% of the Amazonian forest has already been destroyed.

Nasalis larvatus
This animal is also known as the proboscis monkey, because of its long nose. Females live together in groups associated with a male. They live in mangrove forests that grow in swamp areas. Asian and African monkeys are easily distinguishable from South American ones because they do not have a prehensile tail and have a narrower, more elongated nasal septum.

Mangroves
With their intricate tangle of roots, mangroves afford protection to many species of vertebrates and invertebrates. They also protect the land from flooding.

Sumatra rhinoceros
Hunted by poachers for their valuable tusks, which are believed to possess magic and curative powers, the Sumatra rhinoceros is on the brink of extinction.

Borneo tiger
This large predator is nearly extinct and survives only in reserves.

The "forest person"
The orangutan or "forest person" is a splendid large ape that spends most of its time in the trees where it builds shelters with leaves and branches. It feeds on leaves, fruit, berries, and insects. Because of the rapid disappearance of its habitat, it is at risk of extinction.

Great Indian hornbill
While rearing her young, the female hornbill shelters in a tree cavity and seals it with a mud wall. The male passes in food through a narrow hole.

Nepenthes
This carnivorous plant is capable of trapping small insects inside its flower cups.

Rafflesia
The flower of this plant is one of the largest in the world, with a diameter of up to 3 feet.

Islands

There are a number of types of islands, and their origins vary. The so-called continental islands are "genetically" linked to a land mass. They are the peaks of underwater mountain chains protruding from the water and the furthermost points of a continent stretching out into the sea. One example of a continental island is Madagascar, situated in the Indian Ocean. Having separated from Africa in remote times, it developed flora and fauna along different evolutionary lines with respect to the continent. Oceanic islands, on the other hand, derive from volcanic activity in the ocean depths. Underwater explosions can give rise to numerous small archipelagos.

Iceland
The land of "fire and ice," Iceland is the world's most famous volcanic island. It originated about 20–16 million years ago but has still not assumed a stable shape. Eruptions, earthquakes, and lava flows are constantly modifying its contours.

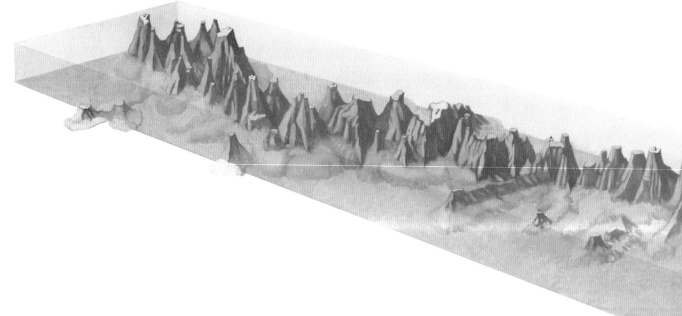

STORIES AND PIONEERS OF SCIENCE

DARWIN'S FINCHES

Charles Darwin's theory of evolution all started with observations made on an island. At the age of 22, the great English naturalist embarked on the Beagle *to start what was one of the most important voyages of exploration in the history of science. One fundamental stop along the way was the Galapagos Islands in the Pacific Ocean. Darwin was especially interested in the finches he saw because their beaks varied according to the island they inhabited. Darwin tried to find an explanation for this, speculating in his diary that a species might have been taken from an originally small number of birds on the archipelago and modified for various purposes. This was the beginning of the theory of evolution.*

Treetops, which are almost invisible from the ground, provide a home for many of the creatures living in the forest, including monkeys, toucans, eagles, and sloths. Insects, reptiles, and amphibians also live and reproduce here and in some cases never descend to ground level. Little light filters through the top layer of foliage, and what does is avidly exploited by smaller trees about 60–90 feet (18–27 m) tall; numerous plant species—orchids, ferns, mosses, lianas—sometimes grow on them. Some of these plants, for instance the climbing ficus, are parasites that gradually strangle their tree host and draw off its sap, eventually killing it. Others, like some orchid species, use the tree only for support.
Often a single plant becomes a miniature "city"

inhabited by various species: A bromeliad growing along the branch of a tree can provide a home, in its long, triangular leaves, for crickets, snails, spiders, and even lizards and small rodents. Soil accumulates on the concave leaves of the plant, permitting the growth of other plants such as orchids or small ferns. Tiny pools of water might also form on the leaves, in which frogs, tree frogs, coleoptorans, flies, and mosquitoes can reproduce. Less than 2% of the light reaches the ground, which is inhabited by the few plants (the kind we see in our apartments) capable of surviving in dark conditions. Large herbivores like tapirs, and powerful predators like jaguars and tigers, therefore have plenty of space in which to move around with ease. ▶▶

Atolls
Atolls are old volcanic islands. The accumulation of detritus, dust, and above all calcareous remains on the craters prevents them from disappearing into the ocean.

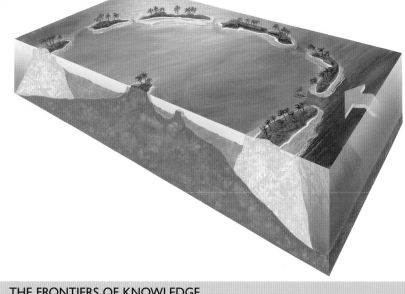

Hawaii
The islands of Hawaii lie in the middle of the Pacific Ocean. They originated as a result of underwater eruptions that created volcanic cones so big they emerged from the water. The material forming the islands has come, down the ages, from a current of molten magma situated beneath the ocean. This is the "hot spot," and its position does not change.

THE FRONTIERS OF KNOWLEDGE

FOREST ISLANDS

The construction of roads, the cutting down of trees to provide space for crop farming, pasture land, and new cities break the great forests into increasingly smaller islands. Ecologists are trying to ascertain the minimum size a forest fragment must be in order to ensure survival of all the species in the ecosystem. In many countries, efforts are being made to maintain "biological corridors" between separate fragments.

Earthquakes

The Earth is rocked every day by about 3,000 earthquakes. Fortunately, almost all of these are very slight and are detected only by measuring instruments. But unfortunately, about 100 times a year, they make their presence felt, often causing serious structural damage and loss of life. A good deal of this intense activity is a sign of what is happening along the tectonic plate boundaries. Plate movements bring layers of rock into contact with each other. To the extent that it is possible, the rock layers are compressed, but a point comes when they cannot be crushed against each other any further, and so they move in search of a new equilibrium. In this way, the energy accumulated up to that moment is released, generating seismic waves and causing the earth to tremor.

Birth of an earthquake
The point underground where rocks begin to break and move against each other is called the focus. This is where the energy that generates an earthquake is released.
The point on the surface vertical to the focus is called the epicenter and is where the greatest damage occurs. Seismic waves arrive here first and then propagate in all directions.

WAITING FOR THE "BIG ONE"

The inhabitants of Los Angeles have been waiting for the "big one" for years. It could arrive at any moment, and according to some experts, it will be the most violent of all time. The city and the whole of the coastal region of California lie on the San Andreas fault, a zone of contact between various segments of an ocean ridge and a portion of the continent. It is therefore a site of tectonic "clashes" just waiting to explode.

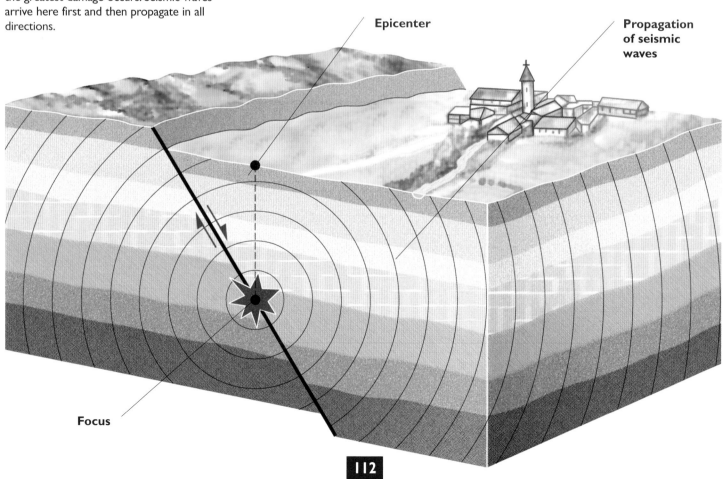

Epicenter

Propagation of seismic waves

Focus

The most devastating earthquakes

1755, Lisbon (Portugal): 30,000 victims. 1976, Tangshan (China): 750,000 victims. 2001, Gujarat (India): 100,000 victims. These are the tragic statistics of some of the most devastating earthquakes in recent history. Ancient chronicles also provide testimony of violent earthquakes striking populated zones. Only in the modern epoch, though, has it been possible to accurately quantify the damage caused by earthquakes, thanks to development of the Mercalli and the Richter scales; these can establish with precision the type of quake and its consequences on the surrounding area.

Fractured rocks

When the rocks compressed by plate movements are subjected to sudden pressure, they break and begin to slide against each other. These fractures, which interrupt the line of the rock strata, are called faults.

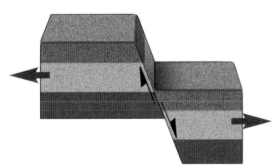

Normal fault
(extension)

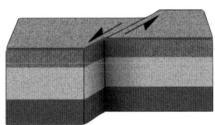

Transform fault
(movement of two blocks against each other)

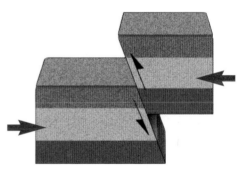

Reverse fault
(compression)

The history of the Earth

It comes as something of a surprise to discover that the rich ecosystem of a tropical rainforest is supported by a thin, extremely poor layer of soil. Indeed, quite a high proportion of the soil on which rainforests grow consists of clay or ferrous blocks that contain practically no nutrients. It is only the rapid and incessant decomposition of the enormous mass of dead leaves and organisms deposited among the branches or on the ground that enables a thin layer of fertile material to form. This nourishes the whole ecosystem. If the forest is cut down and burnt, the layer of fertile material is washed away by the frequent rains and the land rapidly becomes unproductive.

It takes many years for low vegetation to begin to grow again, and many decades before it begins to look like a forest. However, if the deforested area is limited and if it is used only to cultivate crops for a couple of years, it can recover. In the space of a few years, leaves and organic matter are transported by the wind and rain from the surrounding forest, and the area begins to be recolonized. But if the deforested area is very extensive and is used for intensive agriculture, the impoverishment and erosion of the soil soon become practically irreversible. Nothing, apart from a few sparse grasses, will ever grow on the bare clay again. ▸▸

Fires

Fires are a normal part of forest life and are important to ensure certain ecological functions. But when humans set large-scale fires, they destroy the ecosystem. Every year there are tens of thousands of major uncontrolled fires in forests around the world; these cause a dramatic loss of biodiversity and the emission of large quantities of carbon dioxide into the atmosphere, which contributes to exacerbation of the greenhouse effect.

STORIES AND PIONEERS OF SCIENCE

1997–1998: THE YEAR THE WORLD CAUGHT FIRE

After months during which fires blazed continuously in Indonesian forests, at the beginning of 1998 the Amazonian forest started burning as well. Almost 1.5 million acres of savanna and forest in the Brazilian state of Roraima went up in smoke in 3 months, and the native lands of the Yanomami Indians were devastated. Even with international assistance it was impossible to put out the blaze. They were finally extinguished by rain started at the end of March after months of dry weather, a few hours after two Kayapò shamans had, at the invitation of the government, performed a rain dance.

After a fire
Life does not cease after a fire. Although many organisms die, the seeds, microorganisms, and invertebrates remaining in the soil or transported by the wind rapidly build an ecosystem of species. These are known as pioneer species, and they help to retain water and form a layer of organic substances in the ground.

Ecological succession
Once pioneer species have colonized the area, there is a succession of ecosystems. After 10–15 years bushes appear and gradually grow bigger. In the space of a few decades large trees appear, and with them many animals. This is what is known as secondary forest and comprises a limited number of species. Only after dozens or even hundreds of years does the forest return to being a stable ecosystem with a complex network of prey, predators, and decomposers.

Temperate grassland can be found in areas where average temperatures are similar to those found in the temperate forests or Mediterranean regions, but where rainfall is much rarer. This landscape is characterized by herbaceous plants and sparse shrubs and is inhabited by a large number of herbivores (the nilgai in India and the bison in North America, for instance) and their predators (jackals, hyenas, coyotes).

In tropical latitudes, but only where rain is scarce, the dominant biome is savanna, which occupies vast tracts of Argentina, Paraguay, eastern Australia, and above all, Africa. In areas of savanna with no tall trees or hiding places, medium- and large-sized herbivores like gnus and gazelles have evolved.

They live in herds to defend themselves more effectively from predators. Where the savanna does have trees and offers more shelter, small herbivores have also evolved. One example is the dik-dik, which can hide and camouflage itself. The predators also occupy different ecological niches and adopt various strategies. In Africa, hyenas and African hunting dogs prefer to work in packs and divide the spoils, whereas cheetahs and leopards hunt alone.

The land areas where rainfall is very rare and limited (a few inches a year) are covered by deserts. Few organisms are able to adapt to the scarcity of water. This in turn makes these environments even more extreme. ▸▸

Slash-and-burn agriculture
One of the causes of forest fires in developing countries is "slash-and-burn" agriculture. This traditional practice involves making space for cultivation by cutting down large trees, allowing the vegetation to dry, and then setting fire to it. This technique is not harmful if it is practiced by indigenous seminomadic, low-density populations on a small scale. But when it is used for the permanent and intensive colonization of land, it rapidly leads to desertification.

THE FRONTIERS OF KNOWLEDGE

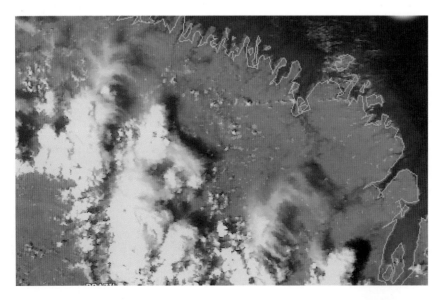

SATELLITE MONITORING OF FIRES

One important instrument in the struggle to put an end to large forest fires is satellite monitoring. International projects to supply maps of major fires have been underway for years. In the Amazon, for instance, the National Oceanic and Atmospheric Administration (NOAA) satellites of the National Aeronautics and Space Administration (NASA) provide detailed images of the state of the rainforests. A new project, called SIVAM, will make it possible to pinpoint not only the coordinates of new fires but also any form of illegal deforestation or aircraft movement. Unfortunately, despite the sophisticated technology, many governments have neither the resources, staff, or at times, will to intervene.

Climatic changes

The average temperature of the planet is rising, although there are still no certain data about how fast this is happening. Some people believe it is just part of the normal geological alternation between hot and cold climates, but the majority of experts argue that one of the main causes is the greenhouse effect. What is certain is that this global warming will already begin to have a serious impact on all living beings within the next 50 years. Possible effects include large-scale migrations of animals and people in some areas, radical changes in vegetation, the gradual disappearance of perennial glaciers, drought, and fires.

STORIES AND PIONEERS OF SCIENCE

ARRHENIUS AND THE GREENHOUSE EFFECT

The great Swedish physicist and chemist Svante Arrhenius (1859–1927) won a Nobel prize for his research into electrolytic disassociation. His hobbies included cosmology, geology, and climatology. As early as 1895, he realized that the increase in the carbon dioxide content in the atmosphere could have serious consequences for the Earth's climate.

The history of the Earth

The scarcity of organic substances in deserts makes the ground almost sterile, so a dense layer of vegetation cannot develop. This in turn causes a dramatic variation in day and nighttime temperatures because the dry air and bare ground are unable to retain the heat. As a result, the temperature may range from 50°C to 60°C during the day to well below zero during the night. Despite the harsh conditions, plants have managed to come up with a way of surviving. Some, like cacti, absorb large quantities of water in the brief moments when it becomes available and store it in their stems. These are covered by a waxy layer that impedes transpiration. Other plants produce drought-resistant seeds that can remain dormant for decades; then, at the

first drop of rain, they produce rapidly growing and flowering plants.

Looking to the future

The history of life on Earth teaches us that living organisms modify the environment in which they live. Even the miniscule cyanobacteria that appeared at the very early stages of life have succeeded in altering the composition of the atmosphere and in shaping the history of evolution. Ecosystems have never been static. They live in a dynamic equilibrium in which species are modified by environmental changes, chance mutations, and natural and sexual selection. ▸▸

What is the greenhouse effect?

The greenhouse effect is an important natural phenomenon because it ensures that the planet has a mild average temperature. The Sun's rays penetrate through the atmosphere to the ground, where they are partly absorbed and partly bounced back up. The presence of "greenhouse gases" in the atmosphere prevents these rays from exiting the atmosphere and redirects them down to the ground, where they contribute to warming. However, the concentration of greenhouse gases is increasing excessively, and with it the temperature of the planet.

THE ECO-FRIENDLY HOME

Architects in many countries are designing eco-friendly homes, buildings capable of reducing CO_2 emissions and their impact on the environment. The orientation of the house, the windows, floors, walls, and cavity walls are all designed to minimize heat loss in winter and provide a cool environment in summer. Natural materials such as stone, wood, straw, and clay are preferred to synthetic ones (resins, insulators, paints), which are often toxic and non-biodegradable. Solar energy supplies heating and electric power. Wastewater is treated with the aid of aquatic plants and earth- and gravel-based filters.

The last major extinction

After the five colossal mass extinctions resulting from geological upheavals or the impact of cosmic bodies, we are now faced, according to many biologists, with a sixth extinction, very different from and even more dangerous than the previous ones. Unlike these, it is taking place in the space of a few centuries rather than over hundreds of thousands or millions of years. And we are the cause of it. Through hunting, pollution, and habitat destruction, *Homo sapiens* is driving thousands of species, many of which are still unknown, to extinction.

Dodo
This large bird, which weighed up to 45 pounds (20 kg), lived on the islands of Mauritius and did not know how to fly. This made it easy prey for European sailors, who used it to replenish their meat supplies. The extermination was completed when dogs, some of which became wild, were introduced onto the island. The last dodo died toward the end of the seventeenth century.

Hadronyche pulvinator
This spider, which belonged to the group of spiders that produce funnel-shaped webs, was a skilled and highly venomous hunter. It lived in Tasmania but has not been seen in years.

STORIES AND PIONEERS OF SCIENCE

THE GREEN REVOLUTION: SUCCESS OR FAILURE?

The green revolution began at the beginning of the 1950s. The idea was to eliminate world hunger by creating new hybrids of corn, rice, and wheat with much higher yields per acre of cultivated land. When people began taking stock of the process in the 1970s, it was clear that yields had increased, but that had only partially resolved the problem. In many regions of Africa and India, access to food was still limited to a minority, the ground was polluted with pesticides and chemical fertilizers, and biodiversity had diminished dramatically because of the large-scale, single-crop production of the "improved" varieties.

The history of the Earth

Even large-scale mass extinctions are an integral part of the history of life because it is thanks to them that new phyla, classes, and living species have developed. However, humans are now capable of modifying the atmosphere in a very different and more profound way. Industrial development has led to major changes in the composition of the atmosphere; the concentration of carbon dioxide has increased substantially, together with that of other gases that exacerbate the greenhouse effect. The result, according to some (but not all) climatologists, is that in the next 50 years the average global temperature will rise by several degrees Celsius, which may have serious consequences for all the world's inhabitants. Whereas cyanobacteria polluted the terrestrial atmosphere over the course of tens of millions of years, humans have done so in less than two centuries. This is too short a time to give the Earth's ecosystems a chance to deal with the problem through evolutionary adaptation.

Human activity has also led, directly or indirectly, to the extinction of numerous animal species. Some have been wiped out though hunting or indiscriminate collecting. Many more have disappeared as a collateral effect of human activity. ▸▸

Moa

This bird was a form of ostrich about 5 feet (1.5 m) tall. It lived in New Zealand and became extinct several centuries ago as a result of indiscriminate hunting.

EXTRACTIVE RESERVES

In order to prevent economic development of areas of tropical forest leading to the destruction of biodiversity and the extinction of plants and animals, experimental "extractive reserves" have been set up in South America. Local inhabitants try to create sources of income starting with what can be extracted from the forest without destroying it. Examples include rubber (obtained by making a notch in the trunk of Hevea brasiliensis), forest nuts, the fruit and oils of palm trees, crafts products, fishing, and environmental tourism. The experiment seems to work well, provided there is initial financial support.

Harpagornis moorei

This bird was a large New Zealand eagle that became extinct at the same time as the moa, which was its sole prey.

Thylacine

Also known as the Tasmanian wolf, this animal was the largest Australian carnivorous marsupial. It became extinct in 1936 due to hunting, habitat destruction, and competition with the dingo, another predator introduced by humans.

Blackfin cisco

Until 1960, this fish could be found swimming in the waters of Lake Michigan and Lake Huron. Like the deepwater cisco, it was very common, and millions of tons were fished each year. Made rare by industrial fishing, the last exemplars were exterminated by introduced species such as the lamprey.

Quagga

This animal was a subspecies of Burchell's zebra and lived in South Africa. Millions of them were killed for their meat and skins and because farmers considered them harmful. In fact, they grazed in the same areas as sheep and goats. The last exemplar died at the Amsterdam Zoo in 1883.

Sustainable development

A crucial concept for the twenty-first century in government circles around the world is sustainable development. This involves looking for ways to use water, energy, forests, and the world's other resources so as to bring about development while ensuring at the same time that they continue to be available for future generations. The only way to achieve this is through international agreements that put a brake on consumerism and the waste of resources in rich countries.

Sustainable forest management
How can we exploit forests without destroying them? One method currently being used experimentally is to selectively cut a small number of trees per acre. Another is to cut in strips rather than a whole large area: The trees downhill are felled first, thus allowing leaves and organic material from the forest above to work their way down and enrich the soil, which can then be quickly colonized by new plants.

The history of the Earth

In Australia and New Zealand, the introduction of species like rabbits and goats has led to the extinction of species that proved unable to compete with the newcomers. Uncontrolled reproduction of new species has also compromised the environment.

Other animal and plant species disappear because of the modification or destruction of habitats. In tropical forests, animals and plants are becoming extinct even before scientists have a chance to study them, and at a rate that is hard to estimate. If past extinctions took place over the course of thousands or millions of years, those due to human activity are occurring in the space of a few decades. Natural evolution does not have the time to produce new species to occupy the ecological niches that are remaining

vacant, and the world's ecosystems are in risk of collapse. For this reason, many experts regard it as a priority for governments around the world to develop common strategies to promote sustainable development. This involves the use of resources—water, energy, raw materials, farmland, forests—at a pace and in a way that will not prevent them from being used by future generations. The human race is at a turning point: We either have to find new ways of inhabiting the planet and modifying the environment or we will disappear in a sixth, mass extinction, caused not by a meteorite, by apocalyptic volcanic eruptions, planetary earthquakes, or variations in the inclination of the Earth's axis but quite simply, and ironically, by human activity.

Landslides and floods

In recent years we have become sadly accustomed to landslides and floods. Often they are the visible and dramatic consequences of an unsustainable management of the environment. Deforestation, erosion, and the channeling of rivers are just some of the causes.

RECYCLING AND REUSING

Sustainable consumption is not only a question of recycling materials. It is also about reusing objects that require a lot of energy to produce or are made from nonbiodegradable materials. Some cutting-edge sectors of research have directed their efforts toward this goal, developing packaging materials that degrade in sunlight, biodegradable plastics derived from plant substances, and products that can be reused and recycled in an increasingly efficient manner.

STORIES AND PIONEERS OF SCIENCE

EASTER ISLAND

Easter Island, off the Chilean coast, offers a dramatic warning of the importance of sustainable development. Archaeologists have succeeded in reconstructing the history of the people that built the gigantic stone faces found on the island. They discovered that the population had condemned themselves to destruction by cutting down the entire palm forest that covered the island. Isolated thousands of miles from the nearest land, with the trees and animals extinct and the soil eroded, the inhabitants were exterminated by famine, cannibalism, and tribal wars.

Index

A

acanthodians **40**
acid
- nitric 103
-sulfuric 103
acid rain 103
adaptive convergence **99**
Africa **39**, 41, **45**, 61, **75**, 81, **83**, 84, **85**, **99**, 110, **115**, 118, 119
- Cape of Good Hope **107**
- Ethiopia 81
- - Hadar 81
- Kenya 106
- - Lake Turkana 82
- - Lake Tanganyika 32
- - Lake Victoria 81
- Sahara, desert of **101**
- Tanzania 106
- - Laetoli 106
- - Olduvai 106
African hunting dogs 106, **115**
Agassiz, Louis 86
agriculture 90, 90, 91, 92
- intensive **113**
albatrosses 100
algae 36, **69**
- single-cell 26, **69**
allosaur **61**
Alvarez, Walter 68
amebas 23
America 30, **83**
- North **40**, **45**, **61**, 75, **83**, 88, 102, **115**
- - Alaska 97
- - Appalachians **45**
- - Arizona 98
- - - California 41, **107**, 112
- - - - Los Angeles 112
- - Canada **45**, 82
- - - Burgess Shale 35
- - - Colorado 60
- - Lake Huron 119
- - Lake Michigan 119
- - - New York 82, 88
- - - - Long Island 82
- - - Purgatory Hill **83**
- - - Rocky Mountains **69**
- - San Andreas fault
- - - shale 35
- - - Sierra Nevada **69**
- - USA 35, 43, **45**, 82, 102
- South 39, **45**, 59, **61**, **75**, **85**, 107, 119
- - Amazon 43, 114, 115
- - Argentina 107, **115**
- - Chile **107**
- - Paraguay **115**
- - Patagonia 60
amino acids 18, **19**, **21**, 21
ammonia **16**, 18
amniotes 53
amniotic egg 50
amphibians **37**, **42**, 42, 46, **47**, 51, **54**, **61**, 72, 93, 95, **96**, 111
Amundsen, Roald 100
angiosperms **62**, 66, 67
animal kingdom 27
ankylosaurs 57
annelids 95
Anomalocaris 34
Antarctic **39**, **45**, 61, **94**, 100, **101**, 101
anteaters 76
anthracite 49
antiseismic constructions 92
ants 67, **94**, **102**
Apatosaurus **61**, 65
apes **83**, **85**
- African 108
- anthropomorphic 83
- Asian 108
- australopithecine **85**, **86**
- catarrhine
- higher 81
- South American 108
aqueducts 33
arachnids 95
araucarias **54**
Archaeopteryx **62**, 70
Archaeopteris 43
Ardipithecus ramidus **85**

Aristotle 104
Arctic 73, **94**, 100, **101**, 101
arctic tern 71
arctic willow **101**
Ardipithecus ramidus, **85**
Arkarua adami 26
Arrhenius, Svante 116
Arthropleura armata 46
arthropods 27, 34, 46, 47
- carnivorous terrestrial **40**
artificial basin 33
Asia 13, 30, 32, 43, **45**, 78, **83**, 88, 90, 102
- Bangladesh 108
- Borneo 95
- China 57, 67, 107
- - Tangshan 113
- Himalayas **75**, 75
- - formation of 32
- India 30, 32, **39**, **45**, 61, 108, **115**, 118
- - Gujarat 113
- Indonesia 17
- - Tambora volcano 17
- Mongolia 90
- - Gobi Desert 60
- Sri Lanka 108
asthenosphere 10, 11, 30
atmosphere **37**, **48**, **94**, 94, 96, 97, 103, 114, **116**, 117, **118**
- primordial 9, 14, 17, 18, **22**
atolls 110
Australia **39**, 41, 43, **45**, 73, 74, **75**, **107**, 107, **115**, **120**
- Ediacara Hills 26
- - fauna of 26, 27
Australian porcupine 74
Australopithecus afarensis 81
autotrophs 22
axis, Earth's **120**

B

Bachofen, Johann Jakob 91
bacteria **21**, 22, 23, **24**, 24, 48, 96
- decomposition of 48
- duplication 23
- genome 23
- membrane 23
- pathogens 101
Baragwanathia 37
bats 62, 74, 76, 77
bears **102**
- polar 101
beavers **94**
beeches **105**
bees 67, 67, **94**
"big one" 112
binocular vision 73
biodiversity 93, 94, 95, **102**, **105**, 108, 114, 118, 119
biological corridors 111
biomes 98, 99, **101**, **105**, **115**
biosphere 94, 95, 96, 97
- cycle of 96, 97
Biosphere 2, 98
bipedalism **85**
birches **105**
birds **37**, 50, 57, **67**, **70**, 70, 71, 74, **78**, 95, **99**, 100, **101**, **102**, 102, 103
- carnivorous 61
- migratory 71, 93
- of prey 93, **99**, **102**, 107
- toothed **67**, 71
bison **115**
biston betularia 29
Black Sea 84
Brachiousaurus **61**
brain 56, **83**, 83
Brazil 95, **107**, 107
bromeliad **111**
Brontotherium 79
broom 66
Buckland, William 60
butterflies **67**, 67, **96**

C

cactus **116**
calcite 12
Cambrian 33, 34, 35, **37**, 78
Canadia 35
carbon 12, 13, 18, 39, 49, 96

- cycle of 96
Carboniferous 30, 42 46, 47, 48, 50
care, parental **77**
Caribbean 95
caribou **102**
carnivores 54, 56, 76, 78
caterpillars 96
Cech, Tom 19
cells **19**, **21**, 21, 24
- chromosomes 25
- cytoplasm 25
- eukaryotic 24, 25
- mitochondria 24, 25, 84
- nucleus 25
- primitive 18, 19, 20, 21, 26
- prokaryotic 24
- respiration 24, **24**, 25
Cenozoic **70**, **75**, 75, 79
cephalaspids 36
ceratopsians 57
Ceresiosaurus 63
Chakrabarty, Amanda 23
Charnia 26
cheetahs 106, **115**
chelonians 53
chemical fertilizers 118
chert beds **69**
chimpanzees 81, 83
chloride, sodium 12
chlorophyll 22, 25
chloroplast 24, 25
chordates 95
cities 90, 90, 92, 93, **94**, **96**, **99**, 111
Cladoselache 41
classification of the species 104
clay 68
Climatius **40**
club mosses, 46
cnidarians 95
coacervates 18
coccoliths 36
cockroaches **96**
cod **75**
coleopterans **47**, 47, 104, **111**
collagen 27
comets 8, 19
competition **53**
conifers **54**, 56, 66, 67, 77, **102**
Cooksonia 37
cooperation 99
- social 90
coral reef **94**
coral polyps **94**
corals 26, 36, 95
core, terrestrial 10, 11, **13**
Coregonus
- *johannae* 119
- *nigripinnis* 119
cork 104
creodonts 78
Cretaceous **61**, 66, **67**, 68, **69**, **70**, 71, 72, 74, **81**
Crick, Francis 19, 20
crickets **111**
crinoids 36
crocodiles 50, 53, **58**, 59, 61
crows **99**
crust, terrestrial 9, 10, 11, 13, 14, 30, 32, 38
crustaceans 36, 95
cryptozoology 75
crystals 12
Cuvier, Georges 59
cyanobacteria **22**, **24**, 24, **116**, **118**
- fossils **22**
cycads 56, 66
cycadeoids 66
Cynognathus 54

D

dams 33
Darwin, Charles 67
Dawson, Charles 82
decomposers 38, 76, 96, 114
decomposition 96, **113**
deforestation 111, **113**, 121
- illegal **115**
dehydration **40**, 42
desertification 115

deserts **47**, 73, **94**, 98, 99, **115**
development
- industrial **118**
- sustainable **120**, 120, 121
Devonian 41, **42**
diamond 12, 13
Diatryma 75
dik-dik **115**
digestion **19**, 96
dingo 119
dinosaurs **48**, 52, 56, **58**, 60, **61**, **62**, 64, 65, **67**, **70**, 72
- carnivorous **58**, **61**, 64, 65
- fossil beds 60-61
- herbivorous 64, 65
- parental care 58
- polar 69
dioxide
- carbon **22**, 22, **24**, 25, 51, 96, 97, 114, 116, 117, **118**
- sulfur 103
Diplodocus 56, 65, **61**
DNA (deoxyribonucleic acid) **19**, 19, 20, **21**, 21, 24, 25, **28**, 69, 75
- double-stranded spiral structure 20, **28**
- mitochondrial 84
- replication **28**
dodo 118
dogs 118
dragonflies 47, 77
drift of continents 30, **48**, **61**, 68
Dromeosaurus 57
drosophila 21
drought **42**, 116
duck-billed platypus 72, 73, 74
Dunkleosteus 40
dust **48**
Dyoplosaurus 57

E

eagle 102, 105, **111**
earthquakes 10, **42**, 44, **67**, 92, 110, 112, 113, **120**
- epicenter 112
- focus 112
earthworms **105**
Easter Island 121
echidna 72, 73, 74
echinoderms 26, 36, **39**, **70**, 95
ecological succession 114
ecosystem **53**, 56, 98, **105**, 106, **107**, 108, 111, **113**, 114, **120**
- artificial **96**
eggplant 66
egg (ova) 51
eggs 56, 58, 59, 74, **75**, 78
elk **102**
embryos **75**
energy
- alternative 49
- electric 117
- solar 117
Entelodont 78
environmental tourism 119
enzyme 19, 20
Eoraptor **61**
equator **45**, **102**, **107**
eruptions **42**, 67, 110, **120**
- underwater 110, 111
extinctions 41, **47**, **48**, **53**, **61**, **67**, **78**, 91, 93, 102, **118**, 119, **120**
- of the dinosaurs 68, 72, **83**
- mass 55, 118, 119
Europe 30, **40**, **45**, 78, 82, **83**, **86**, 88, 97, 102
- Alps **69**, **75**, 88
- England 17, 82
- - Dover, cliffs of **69**
- - - Piltdown 82
- Ireland 94
- Italy
- - Dunarobba 43
- - - Friuli-Venezia Giulia 60
- - - Apulia 60
- Germany 70
- - Frankfurt 76
- - Neander **86**
- Portugal
- - Lisbon 113
- Scotland **40**
Eusthenopteron 44

evolution of species 24, 24, 28, **30**, **58**, **62**, 66, **70**, **75**, **83**, 83, 90, 92, 98, 99, 110, **116**, **120**
- gradualist theory 29
- punctuated equilibrium, theory of 29
exhaust fumes 103
extractive reserves 119

F

farming 90, 92
-intensive 107
faults 31, 113
feathers 57, **62**, **70**
- fossil 70, 71
felines, progenitors of 78
ferns **42**, 46, 56, 66, **105**, 111
- arboreal 46
ficus 67
- climbing **111**
field mice **102**
finches, Darwin's 110
fins 42
fir **102**
- Douglas 102
fires **94**, 114, 116
- forest 115
- slash and burn 115
fish 34, **37**, **39**, **40**, 40, 42, 46, **47**, 51, **62**, 62, 72, 95, 97, 100, 102
- acanthodian **40**, 41
- bony 54
- cartilaginous 40
- fossils 37
- present-day 36
Flood, the 84
flooding 108, 121
flowers 66, 67
- pollination 66
food chain 100, **102**, 102
food pyramid 41, 56, **99**
foraminifera **69**, 70
forest **42**, 46, **47**, 49, **67**, 80, **81**, **94**, 103, 107, 114, 120
- Amazonian, see Amazon
- boreal, see taiga
- conifer **102**
- Indonesian 114
- mangrove 108
- palm 121
- petrified 43
- rain **94**, **107**, **111**, 113
- secondary 114
- selective cutting 120
- temperate 98, **99**, **105**
- tropical 76, 98, 99, **107**, 108, 109, **120**
formaldehyde 18
fossil carbon **45**, 48–49, 97, 103
fossil fuels 49
fossilization 38
fossils 38, 39, 56, 63, 65, 69, **70**, 74, 76, 77, **83**, **85**
foxes 99
- polar **102**
foxgloves 66
Franklin, Rosalind 20
frogs 43, **75**, **96**, 111
fullerene 12
fungi 94, 96

G

Galapagos Islands 110
Gallimimus 57
gametes **30**
- fertilization **33**
- ova **33**
- spermatozoa **33**
gases **10**, **13**, **16**, 16, 17, 18, 19, **22**, **48**, **118**
- greenhouse 117
gastroliths **61**
gazelles **115**
geckos 96, **99**
Gemuendina 40
genes **19**, 20, **21**, 75
genetic code **21**
genetic engineering 69
genetic transfer, horizontal 25
genome 21, 28, 29
geyser 16
giant sloth 91
Giganotosaurus 56, **67**

Ginko biloba 67
giving birth **56**
glaciation, see ice age
glaciers 32, 87, 116
- moraine 87
glands
- mammary **56**, **58**
- sudoriparous **56**
glucose 22, **24**
gneiss 13
gnu 106, **115**
goats **120**
gold 8
gorillas 81
Gondwana **37**, **39**, **45**
granite 12
graphite 12
graptolites **39**
grasses 96
grasslands 78, 79, **81**, **94**, 98, 99, 106, 107, **115**
- desertification of 107
gravity, force of **13**, 13
Great Indian hornbill 109
greenhouse effect 114, **116**, **117**, **118**
Greenland 12, 101
green lizards **96**
gray squirrel 93
grouse **102**
gulls **96**

H

habitats **53**, 95, 102, 105, 109, 119
Haiti 108
Haldane, John 18
Hallucigenia 35
hares **102**
Harpagornis moorei 119
Hawaii 111
helium 8, **10**
Hemicyclaspis 36
Henodus 63
herbivores **40**, 55, 56, **61**, 76, 78, 79, **81**, **111**, **115**
herrings 101
Hesperornis 71
heterotrophs 22
Hevea brasiliensis 119
Holocene 92
hominids 81, 82, **86**
- evolutionary tree 82, 83
Homo
- *habilis* 82, **86**
- *erectus* 84, **86**
- *ergaster* 82
- *rudolfensis* 82
- *sapiens* 82, **83**, 84, 85, **86**, 88, 89, **90**, 92, 118
- - genealogical tree **85**
- - hunting strategies 88, 89
Homo diluvii testis 38
horses 76, **81**
- domestication 90
horsetails 55
hot spots 31
house, eco-friendly
house martins **99**
Hoyle, Fred 19
Human Genome Project 21
hunting 90, **115**, 118, 119
Hyaenodon 78
Hybodus 41
hydrogen 8, **10**, 18, **21**
hyenas 106, **115**
Hypsilophodon 57

I

ice age **45**, 78, 84, 86, 88
- Ordovician **39**
- Würm **86**, 89
Iceland 110
ichthyosaurs **61**, **62**, 62, 63, **70**
Ichtyostega 44
iguanas 59
Iguanodon 56, 57, 59
ilex 104
Indricotherium 79
indris 80
insects 46, **47**, 66, **67**, 67, 77, 93, 94, 95, **102**, **111**
invertebrates **40**, **42**, **47**, **70**, **96**, **107**, 108, 114
iron 10, **13**

irrigation, system of 33
islands 110, 111
isotopes, radioactive 39

J
jackals 115
jackdaws 99
jaguar 111
Japan 67
jaw 37, 40, 41, 42, 54, 55, 56
jays 102
jellyfish 26, 36, 95
Jupiter 8
Jurassic 56, 61, 62, 67
Jurassic Park 69

K
kangaroo 72, 75
Kayapò, indios 114
Kenyanthropus platyops 82
kestrel 99
koala 72
Kropotkin, Piotr 99

L
labyrinthodonts 54
lakes 14, 32, 33, 77
lamprey 119
landslides 121
language 82
larches 102
Laurasia 30, 45
lava 14, 15, 16
lead 8, 39
Leakey, family 106
- Louis 106
- Mary 81, 106
- Meave 82, 106
- Richard 106
Leeuwenhoek, Antony van 22
lemmings 102
lemurs 80, 83
leopards 115
lianas 111
lichens 93, 96, 102
lignite 49
limestone 70
lions 86, 106
lithosphere 10, 11, 16, 30, 32
lizards 52, 53, 96, 99, 111
Lochness monster 75
Lucy 81
lung 51
lungfish 42
Lycaenops 54
lynxes 102, 103
Lystrosaurus 55

M
Madagascar 60, 61, 80, 83, 95, 110
magma 9, 13, 13, 31
magnetic field, Earth's 71
magnolias 67
mammals 37, 50, 54, 54, 56, 58, 67, 70, 72, 74, 75, 78, 78, 81, 101, 95, 100, 102
- adaptive radiation 74
- American 91
- marsupials 72, 73, 74, 75
- monotremes 73, 74, 75
- placentals 73
- primitive 72
mammoths 91
mangroves 108
Mantell Woodhouse
- Gideon 59
- Mary Ann 59
mantle 10, 11, 12, 30
Margulis, Lynn 24
Marrella 34
Mars 8
martens 102
mastodons 91
materials
- biodegradable 117, 121
- synthetic 117
Mauritius, islands of 118
Mediterranean regions 98, 99, 104, 105, 105
Mediterranean Sea 104, 107
- fauna of 104
Mediterranean shrub and wood-land 105, 107
Megalosaurus 60
Meganeura 47

Mercury 8
Mesopotamia 84
mesosaurs 70
Mesozoic 41, 47, 48, 50, 53, 54, 56, 58, 60, 61, 62, 62, 66, 68, 73
Messel, ecosystem of 76, 77
metabolism 34
metals 21
meteorites 8, 13, 14, 17, 19, 68, 70, 103, 120
methane 14, 18
mice 96
microenvironments, artificial 94
microbiology, birth of 22
microorganisms 21, 93, 94, 97, 100, 101, 102, 105, 114
Middle East 84
migrations 116
- of *Homo sapiens* 91
milk 72, 83
Miller, Stanley 18
minerals 12, 34, 38, 58
- crystalline grid 12
- cycle of 97
- lithification 13
mineral salts 102
Miocene 81
moa 99, 119
molecules, organic 18, 19, 20
mollusks 36, 37, 54, 70, 95
- bivalve 67
monkeys 111
monocultural farming 96, 118
monotremes, see mammals
Moschops 55
mosquitoes 77, 111
mosses 96, 102, 105, 111
mouflon 104
mountain chains 32, 40, 67, 75
- underwater 110
mountain francolin, 102
mountains 94, 98, 99
mudskipper 45
multicellularity 30
- birth of 26, see also
  organisms, multicellular
muscles 34, 37
musk oxen 102
mutation 28, 30, 33, 41, 50, 53, 54, 92, 116
- selective pressure 92
Myers, Norman 95
myriapods 95

N
NASA 115
nasalis larvatis 108
nautiloids 39
Neanderthal man 82, 86
nebula, primordial 8, 9, 10
nematodes 95
Neolithic 86, 86, 91
Nepenthes 109
Neptune 8
nests, fossil 58
nettles 96
New Zealand 58, 119, 120
niches, ecological 53, 54, 58, 68, 72, 74, 75, 98, 99, 102, 107, 115, 120
nightshades 66
nilgai 115
nitrogen 39
nitrogenous bases 20, 21, 28
nitrogen oxide 103
Nobile, Umberto 100
North Pole, see Arctic
nothosaurs 62, 63
notochord 34, 37
nuclear fusion 10
nucleic acids 18, 19, 20, 21, see
also DNA and RNA
numbat 73
nutcrackers 102
nuts, forest 119

O
oaks 104, 105
Ocean
- Atlantic 30, 41
- Indian 110
- Pacific 26, 111
ocean abysses 94, 110
ocean beds, primitive 36
ocean ridges 31, 112

oceans 32, 34, 37, 39, 40, 47, 48, 61, 99
- primordial 9, 14, 17, 26, 33, 36, 37
oil 23, 48, 92, 103
- oil fields 48
- oil wells 94
Oligocene 78, 79, 81, 85
Opabinia 35
Oparin, Alexander 18
orangutan 81, 83, 109
orcas 100
orchids 67, 111
Ordovician 36, 37, 39, 40, 48
organisms
- multicellular 26, 30, 33
- photosynthesizing 39
- primordial 14, 16, 17
- replication 20
ornithischians
ostracoderms 36, 39
ostrich 99
Ottoia 35
overpopulation 91
ovules 42
Owen, Richard 60
owl 99, 102
- snow 102
oxidation 22
oxygen 14, 17, 18, 22, 22, 24, 24, 25, 37, 39, 42, 51, 87
ozone 18, 24, 37
ozone layer 24, 40

P
Paleocene 68
Paleozoic 35, 42, 45, 91
palm oil 119
palms 77
Pangaea 30, 45, 47, 54
pangolin 76
panspermia hypothesis 19
Paranthropus bosei 82
parasites 24
pastureland 107, 111, 113
peat 49, 97
peat bogs 97
pelycosaurs 52
penguins 100
peregrine falcon 99
Permian 45, 47, 48, 54, 55, 58, 67
- extinction 48, 55
pesticides 102, 118
Philippines 95, 108
phosphates 20
photosynthesis 19, 19, 22, 22, 24, 25, 25, 96
phyla 33, 118
phytoplankton 97
pigeons 71, 99
Pikaia 34, 37
pines 54, 102
pioneer species 114
placenta 72
placentals 67, 74, 75
placoderms 42
placodonts 62, 63
planetesimals 10
Planetetherium 78
plane trees 67
plankton 69, 100
plants 37, 39, 42–43, 58, 67, 96, 104
- angiosperms 43
- carnivorous 109
- colonizing 105
- herbaceous 96
- gymnosperms 43, 79
- psilophytes 43
- pteridophytes 43
- Rhyniophytes 43
platyhelminths (flatworms) 95
platyrrhines 85
plesiosaurs 63, 70
Pluto 8
pollution 22, 96, 116, 118, 118
pools 102
polar regions 94, 98, 99, 100, 101, 101
ponds 96
poplars 67
poppy family 66

porcupine 101
poriferans 95
potato 66
- cultivation of 94
predators 21, 28, 30, 34, 36, 37, 40, 41, 54, 57, 58, 64, 65, 75, 76, 78, 79, 86, 99, 111, 114, 115
primates 76, 80, 81, 85
- ancestral 83
Probainognathus 56
proboscis monkey, see *Natalis larvatus*
Procompsognathus 56
Proconsul africanus 81
prosimians 83
proteins 18, 19, 19, 20, 21, 21, 28
- synthesis of 20, 21
Proterozoic 26
protoplanets 10
protozoa 22, 23
Pseudomonas 23
pterodactyls 63
pterosaurs 62, 62, 70
public parks 96
Purgatorius 80, 83, 83
Pyrenees 75
python 76

Q
quagga 119

R
rabbits 120
races 40
radiation 13, 28
- ultraviolet 37, 40
radiolarians 69
radius, Earth's 11
rafflesia 109
Rahonavis 61
Ramapithecus 85
Ramphorhynchus 62, 63
rats 96
recycling 121
refuse dumps 96
reindeer 102
reptiles 37, 42, 47, 50, 51, 52, 53, 54, 55, 59, 62, 62, 63, 69, 70, 72, 74, 93, 95, 96, 111
- herbivorous 59
- mammalian, see therapsids
- marine 61
reproduction 28, 30, 40, 42, 75
- asexual 33
- sexual 28, 30, 33
respiration 19, 42, 51, 96
reversal, polar 10
revolution
- industrial 90
- technological 90
- green 118
Rhacophyton 46
rhynchocephalians 58
ribosome
rivers 32, 33, 121
RNA (ribonucleic acid) 19, 19, 20, 21, 21
rocks 10, 11, 12, 13, 17, 24
- age-dating of 39
- attitude 39
- calcareous 61, 87
- clay 61
- cycle of 12
- fractured 113
- igneous 12
- - intrusive 12
- - volcanic 12
- metamorphic 12, 13, 35
- sandstone 61
- sedimentary 12, 13, 61
- Siberian 27
- South African 22
rodents 78, 99, 102, 111
rubber 119
ruminants 78
Russia
- Kola Peninsula 11

S
saber-toothed cat 79
sables 102
salamander 38
salmon 103

sand dunes 107
- erosion of 105
satellite 94, 115
- monitoring via 115
- NOAA 115
Saturn 8
saurians 50
saurischians 57
sauropods 57, 65, 67
savanna 85, 98, 99, 106, 107
saxifrages 67
Scaglia Rossa 68
scale
- Mercalli 113
- Richter 113
scales 50
scaly anteater, see pangolin
Scheuchzer, Johann 38
scorpions 40, 47
- subaquatic 36
Scott, Robert 100
sea elephants 100
seals 100, 101
sea pens 26
sea stars 36
sea urchins 26, 36, 54
seeds 75, 78, 102
segmented worms 27
seismic waves 10, 112
selection
- artificial 92
- natural 28, 29, 41, 50, 54, 92, 116
- sexual 116
sequoia 54, 66
settlements, permanent 90
sewage 96
sex 33
sharks 41
- archaic 54
shells 37, 39, 69
- egg 50
Siberia 97, 103
- Tunguska, forest of 103
silica 69
Silurian 36, 37, 39, 40
single-crop production, see
monocultural farming
SIVAM, project 115
skeletal structures 27, 34, 35, 50
- biomineralization 34
- exoskeleton 27
- shell 27, 34
- - bivalve 36
skuas 100
skull 54, 56, 82
sloth 111
smell, sense of 52, 73, 80
- Jacobson's organ
  (vomeronasal cartilage) 52
snails 111
snakes 50, 52, 53, 67, 96
soil erosion 107, 121
soy, plantations of 107
sparrows 99
spermatozoa 51
spermatozoids 42
sphenodonts 53
spiders 40, 111, 118
Spielberg, Steven 69
spinal column 34, 37
spirochetes 24
sponges 36, 69
Spriggina 27
squamates 53
squirrels 102, 103
- flying 78
starlings 99
stegosaurs 57, 67
Stenodictya 46
Stethacanthus 41
stoats 102
stomata 104
strawberry tree 105
stromatolites 22
subduction 31
suckling 74
sugars 20, 22, 76, 96
sulfur 16, 21
Sumatra rhinoceros 108
Sun 8, 10, 10, 22, 40
swallows 99
swamps 46, 108

T
taiga 98, 99, 102, 102, 105
tapirs 111
tarsier 83
Tasmania 41, 118
temperature regulation 56, 73
teeth 42, 54, 56
termites 94
Tethys Sea 45
Thailand 108
thecodonts 58
therapsids 54, 54, 55, 56, 58
theropods 57
thylacine 119
Tibrachidium 27
tigers 111
- Borneo 108
titanosaurs 61
tits 99
toads 75, 96
- Costa Rican golden 45
tobacco 66
tomato 66
tools, primitive 86
tortoises 50, 53
toucans 111
transpiration 104
tree frogs 96, 111
Triassic 55, 56, 58, 61, 74
Triceratops 56, 57, 67
trilobites 35, 36, 37, 48
tuatara 58
tundra 98, 99, 101
turtledoves 99
turtles 53, 96
Tyrannosaurus rex 57, 67

U
ultraviolet rays 18, 21
umbilical cord 72
uranium 13, 39
Uranus 8

V
variability
- genetic 28, 28, 33
- individual 29
Velociraptor 65
Venus 8
"Venuses," paleolithic 91
vertebrates 34, 36, 37, 37, 40, 42, 44, 47, 50, 54, 55, 108
viburnum 67
virus 25
volcanoes 14, 15, 16, 16, 17, 48
- eruption 16, 17, 44
- explosive 16, 17
- intrusive 16
- lava flows 110
- magma chamber 16
- seismic activity 17
- side vent 16
- vent 16
- volcanic structure 16
Volvox 26

W
walruses 101
warm-blooded animals 54, 56
water 18, 22, 25, 34, 96, 103
- cycle of 97
water lilies 77
Watson, James 20
waxy film 104
Wegener, Alfred 30
whales 97, 100, 101
wild cat 105
Wilkins, Maurice 20
willows 67
wind turbines 49
wing 63, 71
wolf 102
- Tasmanian, see thylacine
wombat 72

Y
Yanomami, indios 114
yeti 75

Z
zebras 106, 119
Zoological Society (London)